MW00898330

THE CHESAPEAKE TALES & SCALES

A collection of short stories

from THE CHESAPEAKE

The world's largest collection of stories in about the people, places and fish of The Chesapeake Bay region

BY KEN ROSSIGNOL

& LARRY JARBOE

With the exception of the non-fiction work presented in the collection of short stories from THE CHESAPEAKE, the collection of short stories is a work of fiction. Names, characters, businesses, organizations, places, events, and incidents either are the product of the author's imagination or are used fictitiously. Any resemblance to actual persons, living or dead, events, or locales is entirely coincidental.

Copyright 1988 – 2015
Huggins Point Publishing LLC
The PRIVATEER CLAUSE Publishing Co. Kenneth C. Rossignol
All Rights Reserved

ISBN-13: 978-1492738961
ISBN-10: 1492738964

ThePrivateerClause.com

Ken@ThePrivateerClause.com

ENTER TODAY with EMAIL address for a chance to win a FREE PAPERWHITE KINDLE or choice of a gift card at Amazon

Visit ThePrivateerClause.com and submit name and email address and win a free Kindle book along with a chance to win a great new Paperwhite or a gift card at the end of our special promotion.

Unlike tablets, Kindle Paperwhite is designed to deliver a superior reading experience.

BE SURE TO SIGN UP FOR OUR EMAIL LIST at

The Privateer Clause dot com

GET ANOTHER BOOK FREE

Available in paperback and Audible at Amazon and retailers worldwide

The Marsha & Danny Jones Thrillers

1 The Privateer Clause
#2 Return of the Sea Empress
#3 Follow Titanic
#4 Follow Triangle – Vanish!
#5 Cruise Killer

Additional books by Ken Rossignol

Chesapeake 1850
Chesapeake 1880
Chesapeake 1910 (coming soon)

Battle of Solomon's Island

Titanic Series

Titanic 1912
Titanic & Lusitania- Survivor Stories (with Bruce M. Caplan)
Titanic Poetry, Music & Stories

The Chesapeake Series

The Chesapeake: Tales & Scales (with Larry Jarboe)
The Chesapeake: Legends, Yarns & Barnacles (with Larry Jarboe)

Non-fiction

KLAN: Killing America
Panama 1914

The Story of The Rag

Leopold & Loeb Killed Bobby Franks (with Bruce M. Caplan)

CHESAPEAKE CRIME CONFIDENTIAL

Coke Air: Chesapeake Crime Confidential

PIRACY and PIRATES – Non-fiction

Pirate Trials: Dastardly Deeds & Last Words

Pirate Trials: Hung by the Neck Until Dead

Travel

Fire Cruise

Cruising the Waterfront Restaurants of the Potomac

The Traveling Cheapskate series:

The Ninety-Nine Cent Tour of Bar Harbor Maine

Boating Chesapeake Bay

DEDICATION

This book is dedicated to our great contributors who have passed on and now compose our Ghost Writing Staff in the vast library in the Heavens:

Fred & Beth McCoy
Jack Rue
Mel Brokenshire
Pepper Langley
Vi Englund
Frank the Beachcomber

CONTENTS

ACKNOWLEDGMENTS

THE REAL AND THE ABSURD ARE OFTEN INTERTWINED AND CONSPIRE TO INSPIRE OUR WRITERS

Hurricanes were strong in the 1930's with a big storm in 1933 demolishing the dance hall and luncheonette at the Point Lookout Hotel. *Photo courtesy of Cue Ball Raley.*

CHAPTER 1
THE OLD HOTEL HAD BEEN "R & R" FOR PENTAGON BRASS

Letter from Point Lookout Hotel

By Alan Brylawski Sr.

The picture of Point Lookout Hotel that was carried in the November issue of The Chesapeake brought back poignant memories that I have actually tried to put out of my mind. The last time I visited the Hotel, She reminded me of a skull looking with sightless eyes across the waters of the Bay. I say 'She,' because to me She was once a lovely old lady sitting there beside the beach smiling at the seagulls and fishermen as they passed in their boats.

Today there is nothing left of what was there. She has been vandalized beyond description. They have stripped Her of everything, from Her furniture to Her kitchen equipment, to Her very doors – even to Her windows, so that now She is a mere hulk of herself and slowly deteriorating – soon to be just a memory.

I try not to think about Her this way, but instead remember the happy times when She was alive with the sound of people laughing and enjoying what She had to offer. It is my hope that maybe my poor excuse for writing will somehow impart to you some understanding and feel for what I perceived Her to be.

She was not the first hotel built on Point Lookout, and she is not as old as she would seem, having been built just after the First World War. I first visited the hotel sometime around 1937-38 and thought She was grand with Her wide double staircase leading to the upstairs from the great oaken-curved desk. I have since learned that business-wise, She was in hard times and had been since the steamboats had stopped calling.

The Second World War was a shot in the arm for Her! During the construction of Patuxent Naval Air Station many a workman was billeted there, since housing in St. Mary's County was practically non-existent prior to building what is now the Lexington Park Hotel and the houses known as Lexington Park (more commonly called 'the flat tops'.)

Those years were the last years in which the Hotel was run year round. As pretty and pleasant as it is down on the Point in summer, it is just as desolate and cold during the winter months when the North East wind whips across the Bay, carrying cold and dampness that can cut to the bone. If there is anyone you know that lived in the Hotel during those years, I would love to hear from them.

Following the Second World War, She had some managers who attempted to run Her successfully, ending up with what was called the 'army' just prior to my abortive attempt. Now in reality, it was an arm of the Pentagon who operated the facility as an 'R & R' for the poor overworked 'Brass.' Being an enlisted man, with my face in the mud during the War while people I didn't know tried to do me bodily harm, it never dawned on me that anyone in the Pentagon needed 'rest and recreation.' I had always thought that the Pentagon WAS 'R & R!' I guess us poor misguided types just never knew the hardships of having a nine-to-five job and being forced to live in or near the Capital of these United States!!

In some fairness to the military owners – they did improve the Old Girl while She was under their command. They installed a sprinkler system, put storm windows on each window, erected a helicopter pad behind the swimming pool (something every little hotel needs,) and saw to it that it was kept in as good of shape as possible. Something I tried to emulate, albeit, with far fewer funds than they had.

The Army-Pentagon decided to sell the facility, because, (we have been told) the 'Brass' came down less and less, primarily because there was no golf course nearby! The poor devils had to drive twenty-one miles to the Pax River Naval installation to play golf!! Moreover, then after an exhausting time on the links, drive another bone shattering twenty-one miles back!! To the best of my knowledge, during that period, no civilian or enlisted men (other than those working for the facility) were allowed on the grounds.

I will not attempt to give you a full history of the old Hotel, rather instead, I will tell you some of the things that transpired while I was manager and gave you an understanding of why it is closed.

How did I become a manager of the Hotel? Good question!! Because, I knew as much about managing a Hotel as I do about constructing an atom bomb! However, Boy!! Did I learn!!

Some business friends from Washington D.C. were persuaded (by me!) to put in a bid for the Hotel; it being up for sale by closed bid. Unfortunately, my friends were the high bidders! (They still own it, to their sorrow.) It was at a lunch meeting we had in The Roost (where else) that they informed me that they had found the man they wanted to manage the Hotel. When I asked who it was, they told me that he was:

1. Hard working (that became prophetic),
2. That he was honest (he has always been),
3. He had a good head on his shoulders if he took this job; he had to be nuts.)

I said GREAT, and WHO is he? AND THEY POINTED TO ME!!! Now I am a sucker for a challenge – and WOW was this one. So I said yes without a second thought (or talking it over with my wife – and the miracle is, is that she is still with me.)

I told my friends (?) that I did not know diddle from squat about running a hotel, and they responded, "One way to learn is to go down there and do it!" And so down I went, taking my wife and our two children with me. We explored what was to be our spring and summer home-away-from-home for the next few years. And what fun that was!!

I had a bunch of keys and nothing else. I did not have a clue as to where the fuse boxes were (and if I found them, I had no idea of what they controlled!) I did not know how to turn on the water – where was the hot water heater anyway?? What we did find that day was a lovely old building with a furnished living room – no, I don't mean a lobby – it was too homey to be a lobby, with its enormous fireplace, its deep comfortable wicker furniture, its lone television set, its woven rugs, and its polished well-worn wooden floor.

The lobby was around the corner, between the living room, and the dining room that could accommodate a couple hundred diners with no problem (except mine). The lobby consisted of the great oaken-curved desk nestled between two staircases that met behind the desk and then swept up to the first floor of rooms.

Next to the dining room on the Bay side was a large cocktail room with an elongated bar piercing the center of the room. All of these were connected by a wide screened veranda starting on the far side of the hotel (where the driveway allowed you to unload and enter the living room.) From there it swept to the Bay and across the face of the Hotel to the cocktail lounge.

Directly behind the dining room was, first, a butler's pantry, and then an enormous well-equipped kitchen, and behind that was a walk-in store-room with freezers and assorted shelves.

Upstairs were fifty (count them) bedrooms of various sizes and shapes. Three had private baths, some rooms had adjoining bathrooms (each bath serving two bedrooms) and some rooms (mostly on the third floor) having no baths – using instead, the two large baths (one for men and one for ladies) at the end of the hall.

The entire Hotel was completely furnished. I was thrilled! Our two sons were unimpressed until they saw the huge 110 feet long, 50 feet wide, and 13 feet deep swimming pool. Jean, my wife, wanted to go home! Sorry Jean!

On the other side of the swimming pool was a long, low building facing the Bay. It contained the bath houses for the pool, a porch that wrapped around the building, a snack bar with grill etc., a dining room (that nobody used, as they liked to eat on the porch and look out on the Bay,) and a game room.

All in all, it was a lot to explore that first day. Now the job facing us was to get the Hotel ready for operation, hire the personnel, advertise, and then sit back and watch the people and the money roll in!!

I guess I will always be a dreamer – 'til next time!

The Point Lookout Hotel. The hotel formerly stood in the area of the parking lot for the fishing pier.
THE CHESAPEAKE photo

The hotel as it appeared in the 1950's when Alan Brylawski was the operator.
Photo courtesy of Jack Witten.

Point Lookout Hotel was located in the area of the parking lot for the fishing pier at Point Lookout. *THE CHESAPEAKE photo by Darin Farrell*

CHAPTER 2 **A FISH STORY**

Fishing's Hot, and that's Nothin' but the Truth

By Lenny Rudow
The Chesapeake

Way back in the late 80's *The Chesapeake* had a writing contest that was won by yours truly, mostly because I managed to tell bigger lies than anyone else.

Little did I know back then that my nautical knowledge would turn out to be of more interest to people than any of the actual literature I'd attempt to write through the years.

So much for art. Still, writing about how and where to fish, recreational boating, and marine electronics is still one heck of a good gig, so I was thrilled when I got a blast from the past and publisher Ken Rossignol contacted me to see if I'd be interested in writing an article for the new *The Chesapeake*.

Yeah, I know—enough expounding, get on to the important stuff, Rudow.

Okay, here goes: The striper season is drawing to a close (December 15 is our last legal day to chase stripers in the bay), but there are still plenty of red-hot opportunities.

Trolling spring trophy spreads of tandem rigs, parachutes, and daisy chains over deep waters in the main-stem Bay is the ticket to fish over 30 inches; run east from Point Lookout until the water depth hits 40 feet, troll to the red #66 marker, turn north, troll up the edge to the Red #72, then turn west and head back for the green 69A. When the bottom comes up under 40 feet, head south for the 66 again.

That pattern is a proven late-season fish-producer.

Light tackle anglers will have a tough time targeting these cows. You can try open water jigging, but it's a long shot; look for gannets, not gulls or terns, which feed on larger baitfish and sometimes indicate bigger fish feeding near the surface.

Use heavy metal jigs like Butterflies or Stingsilvers, drop 'em deep, and consider yourself lucky if you catch one fish for every three or four that the trollers take.

A better bet for light tackle guys is targeting 20" to 30" stripers, which will be corralling bay anchovies and young of the year bunker. You'll find them under flocks of diving gulls throughout the mouth of the Potomac, in the open bay, and in the vicinity of the Gas Docks. Plan on run-and-gun fishing, and make sure you have a good pair of binoculars onboard to help spot the birds from afar.

Satisfied? I hope so because now it's time to shift gears.

In case you hadn't heard, the Gregorian Fault in the Potomac went active again this summer.

The resulting tectonic changes have created a new underwater ridge, three miles due east of Ridge.

The Ridge Ridge, as local scientists have named it, has rapidly resulted in a rigorous realignment of rockfish resources.

On an incoming tide the current sweeps along its base, gets pushed west, hits the drop-off at Butler's Rock, and is forced back to the southeast.

Essentially, it's created a giant swirly.

This new "Chesapeake Vortex," as local scientists have named it, has trapped a plume of warm summer water in place. The elevated temperatures have attracted countless baitfish and many of the bay's summer-time predators, confusing them as they're swept round and round the Ridge-Ridge.

As far as I know no other anglers have taken advantage of this fishing phenomenon yet, but I was there just yesterday. In an hour of fishing, I landed six stripers over 50 pounds, two king mackerel, and a snook.

Lucky for you, out of the goodness of my heart and nostalgia for the old days when I wrote for *The Chesapeake* regularly, I've decided to share this invaluable information with today's *The Chesapeake* readers.

Remember folks, you heard about it here first—and that's nothin' but the truth.

Lenny Rudow has become an accomplished outdoor writer with numerous books and articles on fishing to his name. The St. Mary's College graduate began writing fish stories for THE CHESAPEAKE in 1988 and may conjure future tales of scales.

He is shown here with a King Mackerel.

Cold days of winter see ice reaching out from shore to the river channel.
THE CHESAPEAKE Photo by Ken Rossignol

Only $1

THE CHESAPEAKE

The Original Guide to Fun, Fishing & Nonsense

Announcing: Beneath the Surface Chapter 6

Growing Up in Solomon's Working at the Tomato Factory

by Pepper Langley

see page 12

Island Collides with Tanker

Fun, Fishing & Competition

Pier Tips

MOOSE PIE

Potomac River as the days grow longer and the seasons promise a warm change.

THE CHESAPEAKE photo by Ken Rossignol

Chapter 3
THE CHESAPEAKE ARRIVES IN THE ARCHIVES

One Last Buggy Ride

By Vi Englund
The Chesapeake

For the first time in fifty-two years, I returned to the campus of the University of Northern Colorado in Greeley. It is located just a good eyeful of distance east of the Rocky Mountains, halfway between Cheyenne and Denver.

When I was on the campus, it was a Teachers College, and they had a College High School. I attended high school in 1937 and 38. This was the first year James A Michener joined the faculty with a position in social studies. He remained four years as a professor. My family migrated to California.

After roaming about the world, I made this pilgrimage because Elderhostel offered a week long class on the history of the South Platte.

In the first orientation meeting, twenty-three silver-haired students from all parts of the United States were asked, "Why are you attending this program?"

My response: My mother Elmyra Josephine Paterson was born in Greeley in 1888. Before she was sixteen, her mother and other assorted relatives had made two round trips to Saint Jo, Missouri. Many people were riding by train at this time, but this crew made the journey by covered wagon. They followed the old overland route through Julesburg to the Missouri River. I thought if I learned something about the history of the South Platte I would discover why Grandma was so restless.

The high point of the week was meeting Robert W. Larson, Professor of History. He had just published a book called Shaping Educational Change. It is about the first century of history of the University that was founded in 1889.

I showed him a page from a newspaper printed August 27, 1977. It had an article and picture of James A. Michener and on the same page a picture and article of me autographing my book The Strand. Dorothy Shannon, of *The Enterprise,* had interviewed Michener on the Eastern Shore, and she had written the article about autographing my book.

Professor Larson said, "Come with me. We must have this article and your book in our archives. You are alumni."

We exchanged books. Mine went to the archives, and his came back to St. Mary's.

He said, "Anything else you publish, please send it to the archives."

During the week, I attended informative classes and attended the many interesting functions arranged by Elderhostel. This included a trip to the Rockies to the shadow of those beautiful twin peaks.

I spent much time walking across the campus and re-discovered the yearning for learning that gripped me when I was fifteen. I know now, this yearning was nourished by the atmosphere of this particular school.

One afternoon, Nancy Kisvater, Director of the Elderhostel Program volunteered to take me out to the South Platte.

We found the house I was born, I studied the fields where my family labored. I recalled following the plow and my father, picking up arrowheads. I had a box full. I looked at the river; it is puny compared to the Potomac. However, over the years the Platte has changed the terrain.

The big slough was gone, but enough water remained for fish. I watched the slow-moving carp in the murky water, and the memories went swimming by of life on the sugar beet farm.

On August 4 I received a copy of the August issue of *The Chesapeake.* My article, The Sea, The Boat, and I, was on the front page. It was written at sea on the last sail voyage from the Caribbean to the St. Mary's River.

The Chesapeake traveled by truck from Lexington Park to Washington D.C., by plane to Memphis and plane to Denver, and again by truck to Greeley. All in twenty-four hours by Federal Express.

As I stood by my grandmother's resting place and looked at the stone, I thought of those grueling long trips by covered wagon. My mother described to me the hardship and the time – the long slow time of those journeys.

Moreover, then I thought of another story. The Doctor had told my grandmother she was going to die. A few days later she looked up at my father and made her final request.

"Henry, will you take me for one last buggy ride."

Over a half century, the Platte has changed the terrain of the river bed. Over a half century, the time has changed the terrain of my thinking. I feel a kinship with those pioneer people who struggled for their life on the Great Plains.

Maybe someday some grandchild will wonder why Grandma was going to sea in a sailboat when everyone else was zooming around in a jet.

So I took the August copy of ***The Chesapeake***, with my article on the sea and placed it in the archives of the James A. Michener Library.

I only hope when my time comes that I can say with gusto, "Please take me for one more buggy ride." Or in my case it might be – one more sail – for I love the sea.

The Kalmar Nyckel sailing on the Potomac River. THE CHESAPEAKE photo

CHAPTER 4
FROM SOLOMON'S TO BEACHES OF NORTH AFRICA

By John J Peterson
The Chesapeake

(Editor's Note – This is the first in a series of reflections on the role of the Solomon's as a training base for American troops who would take part in the assault on Hitler's Europe.)

There are still some remembrances to be found around the fringes of the Calvert Marina attesting to the history of the part Solomon's played in supporting the American war effort against Nazi Germany in World War II. However, it is not likely that these man-made mementoes, constructions of a previous era, will long last as progress continues to eat away at what was one of the country's primary amphibious training bases almost a half-century ago.

Although its lifespan was relatively short-lived 1942 to 1945. During its three-year lifetime, approximately 70,000 servicemen received their specialized amphibious training at the Navy base. The new base got off to a rocky start with nearly 15,000 men occupying facilities designed to accommodate less than 10,000 by late 1942, and suffering a lack of formal classes, books and equipment with some men resorting to using handheld flashlights for blinker drill.

With the assumption of command in October 1942 by the original base training officer and many of the major organizational quirks behind him, improvements were quick to come. According to documents of the Naval Historical Center in Washington, D.C., "Until the end of 1942, Solomon's Island was a scene of continuous and often desperate improvisation, morale was low because the amphibious forces were often looked upon as the 'Siberia of the Navy', little liberty was granted (probably because there was no place to go and no transportation to get there), water was in short supply, housing was unspeakable, the land muddy, small stores carried few items and transportation non-existent. Adding to the confusion and low morale, was the fact that most of the initially assigned officers were fresh out of college lacking in knowledge of seamanship, navigation, or gunnery.

Beginning in October. However, written regulations were provided, regular classes instituted, streets were graded and paved, more Quonset huts and barracks were provided the result of all being a considerable increase in morale. Navy documentation attributes much of the disorganization to the fact that the base grew too rapidly with as many as 18,000 men transferred or reassigned in the space of one week.

In addition to growth problems in the establishment of an amphibious base, there was the additional trial and error evolvement of basic land warfare into a combination of sea assault and land warfare. During World War I there were the ports of England and France from which masses of troops could be moved into battle and to engage in primarily trench warfare, thousands of men fighting bloody battles over sometimes but a few feet of ground which was often bloodily recaptured.

With World War II, allied armies would first have to secure footholds on the continent of Europe and North Africa as they leapfrogged island to island throughout the Pacific Ocean once Japan entered the war. The concept of amphibious warfare, long within the expertise of the U.S. Marine Corps, was now to involve the mass transport of hundreds of thousands of Allied soldiers into positions from which they could attack the enemy. Increased training in amphibious warfare was necessary.

As for the onslaught on Europe, Allied plans called for the seizure of a beachhead in France late in 1942 by "Operation Roundup" aimed at crashing through German defenses and knocking Germany out of the war. Also under consideration was "Operation Torch", a landing on the coast of Morocco in North Africa. While the Soviets were favoring the assault on Europe, the British favored the North African assault. With the delay of Operations Sledgehammer and Roundup, and the determination that the attack on North Africa be scheduled in November, the latest date possible because of expected severe weather conditions, the Navy was required to provide some 3,000 trained crewmen in a period of two months.

Initially, amphibious exercises had been conducted on New River, North Carolina, and Cape Henry, Virginia, which, however, were not considered satisfactory for several reasons among which, were lack of protection from U-boats roaming the Atlantic, differences in service doctrines, and inter-service rivalry in matters of command. The consequences were the decision that operations under the auspices of the Navy, such as the Pacific Theatre, would be trained on the West Coast, while those lead by the Army in the Atlantic would be trained at Solomon's.

The Commander-in-Chief Atlantic Fleet recommended the vicinity of Cape Henry and between Solomon's Island and Cove Point offering proximity to Norfolk and protection from the marauding U-boats. The Marine Corps Maj. Gen. Holland M. Smith concurred. Sites were inspected with a final selection of approximately 117 acres of government-owned land at Solomon's, on the peninsula bounded by water on three sides, Mill Creek, Back Creek, and the mouth of the Patuxent River where it emptied into the Chesapeake Bay. Legend has it that the parcel of land was named after a Capt. in Solomon's who opened an oyster cannery there following the Civil War.

The foregoing is but a brief overview of the importance this relatively small spit of land played in preparing American forces for their assault on the Axis-held continent of Europe. Greater detail will be described in future issues. I am obliged to Mike Walker of the Navy Historical Center in Washington D.C. and Paul Berry of the Calvert Marine Museum for their assistance in leading me in the right direction during my research. It should also be noted that the Museum offers "Cradle of Invasion" for sale in its gift shop. It is an excellent account of the Navy Amphibious Base.

Higgins boats are landing troops on Normandy Beach on D-Day in 1944. U. S. Navy photos

The remains of Bowens Inn after the disastrous fire of 2006. The old hotel and bar was the center of off-duty life on Solomon's Island during WWII.

CHAPTER 5 ADVENTURES AT THE DOCK

By Mark Robbins
The Chesapeake

Almost everybody I know thinks that the adventures in sailing happen on the high seas or in distant, exotic ports beyond the far horizon. Of course, a lot of the experiences of sailing happen like that, but not all the adventures of sailing happen in these places, not by a long shot.

Here are two of the wackiest sailing adventures I ever had, and they happened right at the dock where I was tied up.

The first and the most outlandish was the strange case of the noisy nightmare. Now most people think of a nightmare as a bad dream, but that's when you spell it out all as one word. When you use two words like I just did, you're talking about a horse at night, and that's exactly what happened.

It was in a marina at a creek somewhere in Virginia I forget exactly where. Across the creek was a farm where horses were bred, raised, and sold. There was also a tippler there who, to avoid driving while under the influence, rode his horse nightly to the local tavern. When he rode to the tavern, he rode up the creek to a bridge, then on to the tavern. So far so good. The ride to the tavern didn't bother anybody. It was the ride home that immortalized that dipsy jockey in my memory.

When our boozing Bronco was finished at the tavern and was all fired up with the booze in his belly, he always took the shortest route home which was a straight line drawn from the tavern to the stables on his farm. This line ran right through the marina where I was. That's why I awoke several nights in a row about 2 a.m. with a vague impression that I had dreamed that a galloping horse had just ridden by my sailboat. At first I dismissed the sound of a galloping horse is a dream or a nightmare. However, it happened every night; first there was the distant beat of hoofs, then the thunderous sounds of the hoofs as the horse galloped down the dock, then an eerie cry of GERONIMOOOOOOOOO; then complete silence.

After a few nights of this, I couldn't sleep. I was afraid to go to sleep lest I dream again of the nightmare. That's why on my last night in the marina; I saw it all with my own eyes.

It was about 2 a.m., as I was walking on the dock because I couldn't sleep. I heard the distant beat of hoofs. Presently a horse and rider appeared approaching the dock at full gallop. That man could ride a horse like few men I have ever known. He was riding hell for leather straight toward the dock. I stepped behind a piling to avoid being trampled as the dappled mare rode past me at a breathtaking pace. At the end of the dock, the horse leaped far out into the creek. After the horse and rider had leaped from the dock and before they landed in the water in the creek, the rider cried in a mighty voice GERONIMOOOOOOO. Once in the creek the horse, with the rider still in the saddle, swam slowly to the far shore then walked at a subdued pace from the shore to the stables.

To tell you the truth, it was one of the doggonedest things I ever saw, but later that day when I recounted the story of the galloping horse, I found that I was the only one at the marina that was surprised. It seemed that the rider, an ex-paratrooper, (that's why he yelled Geronimo because that's what paratroopers yell when they jump out of the airplane), was owner of the farm across the creek and was an excellent horseman. He worked hard every day, and he made his horse farm pay, but he liked to drink every night – always from 10 p.m. to 2 a.m. I just wish somebody had told me about the nightmare when I first arrived at the marina. It would have saved me a lot of sleep.

The other dockside adventure was just as wacky but, unfortunately, there was a loss of valuable property and several on the dock at the time were almost killed, but happily they were able to escape injury.

It all started when the yard hand arrived at the head of the dock in his golf cart to work on a boat. However, this day by itself was not at all unusual or in any way suggested the incredible sequence of events that was about to unfold to the harrowing surprise of all the dock at the time.

The workman's golf cart was, like I said, parked at the head of the dock. In a nearby field, a young boy was playing with his motor-powered model airplane that he flew in circles around himself at the end of a long control cord.

Events began to happen quickly when the control wire parted. The model airplane, now unrestrained, headed for the golf cart at the head of the dock. The golf cart started when the model plane crashed into the driver's seat. The cart moved slowly at first because it was heavily loaded with tools of all sorts, including many expensive power tools and electronic meters.

As the cart headed for the open end of the dock with gathering speed, it became a real danger to all in its path. Most of the people on the dock saw that the cart was a runaway and rather than take the chance that it might turn at any time and strike them jumped into the creek. At least six people on the dock and one stray dog thought that being in the creek was safer than being on the dock.

The golf cart turned neither to the left nor the right, but ran straight down the dock and plunged at top speed into 24 feet of blackish water carrying all of the unfortunate workman's tools that he had collected over the years in working on boats, as well as the crashed model airplane that was still in the driver's seat.

At the time it happened, nobody thought it was amusing, but later that evening when all the sailors on the dock talked about the runaway golf cart, the whole event seemed funnier and funnier. After a few beers, everybody thought it was about the funniest thing that had ever happened.

Well maybe the sailors thought it was funny, and maybe even the people who had jumped into the creek thought it was amusing in looking back on it. No matter how funny others might have thought the whole thing was, there were two who never would think it was funny; the workman who lost his tools and the young man who lost his expensive model airplane.

I almost forgot the stray dog. It was never seen again on the dock. He no doubt refused to return to that dock because he thought all the people there were the craziest people he had ever seen.

A boat dredges for oysters on the Chesapeake Bay.
THE CHESAPEAKE photo

Cobb Bar Light once stood at the entrance to the Wicomico River and guided boats in from the Potomac to Cobb Island.

CHAPTER 6 SPACE FISHERMEN

By Cap'n Larry Jarboe
The Chesapeake

One evening, while watching the movie "Space Cowboys" about a group of old timers who took a mission on the space shuttle, I was reminded of the day when we caught a couple coolers full of fish from directly beneath the external fuel tank of one of the early space shuttles.

Capt. Tom Mulcahy and Capt. Jerry Theiss was joint partners of three boats in the Majestic Fishing Fleet that operated out of the Holiday Inn Docks in Key Largo. Capt. Tom also had his own boat (that I recall being a Bertram). He also had a significant scar on the front of his body that ran from his shoulder to his groin. Prior to his joint business venture with Jerry, Tom Mulcahy was an Eastern Flight Ops employee who survived Flight 401 that crashed into the Everglades on December 29, 1972. I hope Tom will write his story of that event one day for readers of the CHESAPEAKE. He is a remarkable man.

In mid-June of 1979, Capt. Tom had invited a group of fellow U.S. Coast Guard licensed captains on a dolphin (mahi-mahi or dorado, NOT Flipper) fishing trip. To my recollection, Capt. Tom and Capt. Jerry was joined by Capt. Fred Wheeler, fellow good pirate Dan LaCross, and I. Dan was the only guy on the boat who did not have a tonnage license or run fishing trips for a livelihood.

Generally speaking, June is a good time to troll for dolphin in the blue waters of the Gulfstream off the reefs of the Florida Keys. On this particular day, the ocean was nearly flat calm that is good for fishing but sometimes not so good for catching. Our rigged ballyhoos skipped on the surface without a bite as we worked from Sargasso weed patches to floating debris looking for schoolie dolphin. We tried trolling toward the lone frigate birds hovering overhead that usually follow fish. By late morning, we had not caught a single fish.

Far out in the deep water there was a strange looking apparition on the surface of that flat calm sea. It looked like a big barn or Quonset hut on a barge with a tug floating beside it. We heard on the VHF radio that the tug had broken down while pulling a large tow.

We discussed our fishing strategy. The only non-captain among us figured out the game plan for success.

Dan said, "Dolphin like to hang out in the shade. It looks to me like every dolphin in this part of the ocean is hanging out under that big floating barge." We looked at each other incredulously. Quickly, we pulled in our lines. Capt. Tom planed his boat toward the drifting vessels.

As we slowed and maneuvered closer, we saw the drifting barge held a giant hollow cylinder. The crew of the disabled tug pointed toward the massive school of dolphin that was between the tug and tow. They had been trying to catch them but had no bait for their hand lines.

The captain of the tug directed us between the tug and tow. All lines went down with fish on. We milked the school by keeping one dolphin in the water while we cast ballyhoo chunks to the other fish that stayed with our drifting boat. After three passes, we had loaded both coolers with fish. Capt. Tom pulled his boat close to the tug and directed us to toss a few choice dolphins to the tug's cook. We also bagged and threw the rest of our ballyhoo to the tug's crew so they could join the fun.

We questioned what was on board the barge. The captain of the tug explained that his tow was the fuel tank for the space shuttle. Another tug had been dispatched to complete the voyage to Cape Canaveral. Help was on the way, so we headed for the dock to filet our catch. Later, I learned that the shuttle tanks were built by Lockheed-Martin in Louisiana and delivered to the Kennedy Space Center by tug pulled barge.

Many people have questioned the veracity of my fishing stories, especially Denise at Thompson's Seafood, but there are four captains who are still alive today who will testify how we caught a boatload of dolphin from beneath the fuel tank of the space shuttle.

Moreover, still living in Key Largo, there is one non-captain named Dan LaCross, who showed all those fishing captains (including me) where the fish really were.

Cap'n Larry Jarboe at the helm of a charter boat in the Florida Keys.

CHAPTER 7

ELECTRICITY ARRIVES IN SO. MARYLAND

I was talking to someone the other day about when I first took over Pt. Lookout Hotel. I spoke of the complexity of the electrical system at the hotel and how nobody told me where anything was. When I walked in, there were quite a number of boxes, some with as many as twenty or thirty switches on them, and they were scattered all over the place. I had no idea what they did --- what they turned on --- what they turned off. It took us quite a few weeks to figure out the wiring of the hotel.

Never really did figure it all out completely, but we were able to get by.

Then I got to think, the hotel was built in 1928-1929, so the wiring in the hotel had to be done quite some time after that.

Not only was there no electricity in the lower part of St. Mary's County, but rural America was way behind in electricity.

The cities had electricity for as long as I can remember. Someone said that I go back a long way. Not quite true. Being born in 1921, at least they tell me I was born on March 3, 1921 because I was just too young to remember.

Being born then and living most of the year in Washington, D.C., spending my summers down in Southern Maryland. I had considered myself to be more Southern Maryland than Washington, but Washington, D.C. had electricity. I assume most big cities did some time ago.

Rural America and Southern Maryland was a part of rural America even though we were very close to the capital; we did not have electricity. Moreover, it was back in 1935 that Franklin Delano Roosevelt established the REA, better known as the Rural Electric Administration. He established that because there was no electricity in rural America. Its purpose, so they tell me, was to get commercial interest to invest in electrifying America.

Unfortunately, that didn't work, or maybe, fortunately.

And so in a lot of rural areas as it was down here in Southern Maryland. The people got together and formed a co-op. The first co-op, if I remember correctly was a Tri-County Electrical Cooperative Association, and they were formed sometime in 1937. My father was one of the first one hundred people to join the co-op.

In 1938, we obtained electricity. We were, at that time, living in an area called Tompkinsville, Charles County, on the Wicomico River. It was rather interesting because my father was with Warner Brothers. He wasn't a movie star. He took care of the real estate for the Warner Brothers Company on the East Coast, and he lived and worked in Washington, D.C.

Prior to going with Warner Brothers, he and my grandfather built what is now called The Warner Theatre at 13th and E Street, and the office building that surrounds it.

Originally it was called the Earl Theatre, and of course it started out very, very early in the 1920's as a Vaudeville theatre and then, of course, went to the silent movies and then movies with sound and so forth came in and now it is a prime theatre to this day.

My earliest recollection living in Charles County was on the Wicomico River.

Oddly enough, we had electricity but the rest the rest of the county did not.

Father, being from the city and being used to electricity, and one of my uncles, well, he really wasn't an uncle, but we called him uncle, his name was Uncle Edward. He was the chief electrician at the Earl Theatre, and he handled all the stage work.

I do recall going backstage and seeing that. Today, I think little switches handle everything and you sit at a small console and handle all the electric, but in those days, the switches were enormous. They were huge double throw switches, and when you would throw a switch, sparks would fly.

The lights were huge, and it really took something to handle all that electricity back there.

My recollection of that was rather impressive, but my uncle, Uncle Edward, used to love to come down to Tompkinsville and spend some time with us. I don't know if it was his idea or not, but somebody in the family decided we were going to have electricity.

We had bought an old farmhouse, which was on the water, and I do remember when we had no electricity. I don't remember where we got it, but I can remember the Coleman lanterns, and I can recall that we had a spring. We used to cool our food and our watermelons and such as that in the springhouse. Just set them in that cold water, which would come up out of the ground. In those days, it was a true artesian well as to say it actually flowed; you didn't have to have a pump to pump it up.

Well anyways back to the electric.

My father decided that he was going to have electricity. He built a little shed about two hundred or three hundred feet away from the house. In that shed he put a one-horse power, not on horsepower, one cylinder engine what similar to the Palmer Engines that the Crabbers used to use. You could hear them, back in those days, going down the road.

They would have four revolutions and hit on the fourth and not hit on the third, so it made a rather peculiar noise. This one-cylinder engine was hooked to a generator and to create electric they ran this all day long. It charged some batteries, thirty-two to be exact. The batteries were huge. They were glass batteries so you could see them bubbling.

Again they were really the batteries, and if you can imagine thirty-two of the big batteries on the shelves in this shed with this one-cylinder engine going bang! Bang! Bang! All day long charging these batteries.

Each battery in turn would generate one volt and a thirty volt systems. Today we have what is known as AC Alternating Current. Those days, we had DC or Direct Current just like you have with the dry cell batteries today, or a battery in your car was the same sort of thing. We generated thirty-two volts. I don't know what the interference was, but we could use that electric in the evening to run a few lights, and we could use it to have a pump for the water system.

That allowed us to have indoor plumbing. I suspect in Southern Maryland for the time we had it because I believe we had it from 1926 on. We had something that most homes in rural America, particularly Southern Maryland didn't have indoor plumbing in the early or mid-twenties.

By that time, we also had a refrigerator, but not like the refrigerators you have today. This was not run by electricity. That was run by a rather odd thing. It was a Kegometer.

I believe they are still manufactured. They are used in so- called emerging countries, which might not have electric. They run off of heat. I'm not going to go into how they work because I'm really not sure of the exact theory of it. I know they had no moving parts, absolutely no moving parts. They had a small flame, and they transformed liquid into gas and back into a liquid again which create a cold.

Ours was run by coal oil, now called kerosene, as was our stove. That was the latest for the country in which we had a coal oil stove that was supposedly a step up from the wood stove. Certainly was a little bit cleaner and took a lot less effort which had to go by the kerosene. We had radios that were run on batteries called Kent Atwater radios. They had dials that must have been about 4 inches in diameter and looked like an amazing gang of things in there and was very impressive looking. Of course, every we heard was AM band radio. We pulled in a fantastic amount of static.

(This column by Alan Brylawski is from March of 1990. Alan has proven that he can indeed outlive his detractors; the author is now 94 years old and will be updating his columns soon. Alan is a longtime local Realtor and former owner of the old Mr. Donut in Lexington Park, as well as the Baskin-Robbins, and during the sixties operated the Point Lookout Hotel. His dear wife Jean passed away in January 2011.)

The Warner Theatre in Washington, D.C.

Aunt Bessie and Helen Morris next to a Model "T" Ford in this photo courtesy of Malcolm Morris.

CHAPTER 8 OUR SHORE

Writers often speak of the influence in one's life in living near one of nature's phenomena, a forest, a mountain or a plain.

Ours is our creek and river shore, ever-changing, never-changing. Over the years, many happenings have occurred there.

I remember back before WWII when I was using my two young Belgian horses to cultivate a cornfield along the shore.

I had them hitched to a new sulky cultivator and we were doing a good job. The fenders were set just right and the worked earth was slipping nicely under them and covering the small grass and weeds.

I was proud of my team, I had broken them myself. They reminded me of two big teddy bears, gentle but powerful. At the end of the field, I glanced out to the river. I could not believe my eyes for there was the biggest battleship I had ever seen. She was swinging at anchor in the channel a short distance above the mouth.

I thought she must be the new ship that had been building at Norfolk. She proved to be and was named the "USS South Dakota."

I noticed at once that she was not like the WWII battleship since her bow flared upwards like a cruiser's. Just seeing her there made me feel proud. Soon things would rapidly change.

It would not be long before that huge dreadnaught would no longer be peacefully at anchor with her great 16 inch guns unfired but be in the midst of the greatest war in history. I, too, no longer would be guiding my colts around in a cornfield but would be in the midst of the strife, wearing naval insignia.

Some years later I would be back again on my farm. I would have several children and they too would be influenced by the shore.

I remember one day when it was said "someone pulled the plug in the Chesapeake Bay." The wind had been blowing for several days, pushing water out of the Virginia Capes. The tide fell lower and lower. It was winter time and very cold. My youngest girl, in her early teens, said, "Dad, let's go down to the river and dig some mannose."

Mother, my daughter, my littlest boy and I were all for it.

Soon the tractor and cart were ready, shovels, buckets, and baskets were piled on.

Dressed warmly we made for the beach.

We rode right out on the sand and stopped where we knew the mannoses were. There was no water, where it usually flowed; the wind had blown it all out. We searched for the little air holes that told us the clams were beneath. We dug quickly and the clams fell into the holes.

The strong wind lashed at us and we took turns resting behind a sand ridge on the bank.

In no time, we had over a bushel of those luscious clams.

What a feast!

Mother fixed them in every conceivable way.

We had succulent steamed ones, dipped in hot butter and spices. Some were fried. Best of all was the Mannoses soup, a real Maryland Clam Chowder, rich and nourishing.

Our good friend John Garner used to say mannose soup just made you feel warm and happy inside.

One winter I got a small used gill net from Mr. Forrest at Ridge.

Early that spring, I set it offshore, close to where I could drive my car. Each morning, I would rise early and take a large bath towel with me, undressing in the car; I'd wade out and fish the net. Usually, I would get four or five rockfish, each about three pounds. One day when I arrived, my old net was torn to pieces, holes all through it. A school of large fish must have been the culprit. I was not really too disappointed. I was a little tired of my morning cold-water bath.

Some years back there was a significant amount of sea grass in the shallow waters at the upper end of our shore.

At the right tide, one could dip a basket of crabs in no time.

The children could easily fill a big plastic trashcan full and have to quickly bring it up to the house so the bottom ones wouldn't suffocate. Out usual method of crabbing was using a trotline in our creek.

We had a private oyster bar there, which we planted and where we harvested our oysters. All in all, we made good use of the bounty of the sea.

Our shore is uninhabited and wild and we do have unusual happenings there.

One day we heard that some poor man had been lost in a small boat at Pt. Lookout. His skiff was found washed up on the Bay shore, but he was missing.

Some days later on, some of our children were walking our beach, some three and a half miles above the Point.

My youngest son, four years old, ran ahead of his brothers and sisters then came rushing back, yelling, "There's a dead man on the beach."

The others took a quick look and raced for home. We could hear them calling as they approached the house and feared something terrible had happened to them. The sheriff was notified and after his investigation, called the undertaker.

Two of my high-school boys went down with them and helped roll the body into a plastic sheet and put it on a stretcher.

Not being used to such a job, they got the back end of the load to carry. The Undertaker gave them five dollars for their help, but they vowed, never again to be inveigled into such a task.

Some of us worried that this affair might affect the four-year-old tender of the body, but we were reassured to hear him the next morning imploring his sister, "Let's go down to the beach and hunt for another dead man."

On a fall morning a few years ago, there was a knock at our back door.

There stood a scarecrow of a man, bearded, disheveled and wearing a well-worn slicker. He said, "I have my boat on your shore. I'm looking for a store."

We were glad to point our Buzzy's Country Store at the end of our lane.

Returning later, he asked for permission to sleep on the beach. It was cold and rainy out.

We didn't think much of this and suggested he go up the river to Wynne where he could get some conveniences.

He told us he was in a canoe with a sail and started at the South Branch of the Potomac and had got to Point Lookout, but the waves were so high his canoe was swamped. My wife felt sorry for him but didn't relish feeding him in the house. She packed a bag with meat, bread, eggs and fruit and a jar of hot coffee and off he went.

I believe he was somewhat similar to the poor wretch had been washed up on our shore, lacking something in as the kids say "The upper-story."

A few days later, I ran into Captain Bruce Scheible and asked if had seen any such character over at Wynne.

He asked, "Fred, you mean that 'bag of dirt?'" "Yes, I saw him. He used my phone and the next day an elderly couple in a Cadillac appeared. They rented a room in my motel and soon he was in there with them. Next morning, at first light, I heard some banging near our trash dumpster. The elderly gentleman and a now somewhat cleaned up man were busy, breaking up the canoe with an axe and depositing the debris in the dumpster. When the elderly man checked out, I asked him, "Is this something like the Prodigal son, and he sadly nodded his gray head."

One Christmas we had taken the children up to their aunts to have Christmas dinner and to see what Santa Claus brought them at Glem Coy in Prince George's County. It was a bitter cold evening and we were driving a Jeep station wagon with no heater. One of the aunts filled a large milk can with hot water and covered it with an old comforter. The children lay on pillows and cowered around this and kept warm on their way home.

We arrived well after dark and, of course, they were all asleep when we got to the farm and we carried them in one at a time. I kept hearing gun shots from the beach and thought someone was into geese there, but then I heard calls of distress, maybe a mile off. The ground was frozen hard, so I drove the Jeep down over the fields to the water. I heard voices coming from a duck blind off shore in the river. They called that their boat was washed from them.

I didn't see any boat.

They then shouted for me to call Roache Clarke's Bar and get somebody to pick them up.

Roache was glad to hear from me for there at his place were two ladies anxiously searching for their husbands, but he didn't name them.

Evidently he got in touch with Scheible's and the stranded hunters were rescued by a party boat. Several weeks later, someone informed me that they were talking to Mr. So and So and he said he would never forget what I had done for them, since neither of them could swim, and the waves were getting higher and higher and they had used up all their shotgun shells and all of their Christmas spirits.

One winter, the river froze up all the way to the channel and the wind piled ice cakes one on top of the other and blew them ashore.

Some piles of ice were over ten feet high.

The children were delighted with the crystal blocks, glistening in the sun and decided to explore the shoreline. They walked way out on the ice and, of course, one had to fall in. She was able to scramble out and roll on the ice and reach her sister's outstretched hand. The northwest wind was blowing and it was well below freezing.

The oldest girl had her take off all her clothes immediately and gave her some of her own outer garments. They jogged over a mile to the house. I scolded the one who ventured out too far and fell in, and praised the common sense of her sister, who kept her warm and probably saved her from pneumonia.

I could write of many more instances when someone of ours had helped folks stranded on the shore and of the boys hunting and trapping experiences, but this is sufficient.

Now our children are grown and all have homes of their own. When they come to visit, they put their luggage in the front hall, leave their spouses and children to get settled and are off to the haunts of their childhood along the water edges of our tidewater creek and river.

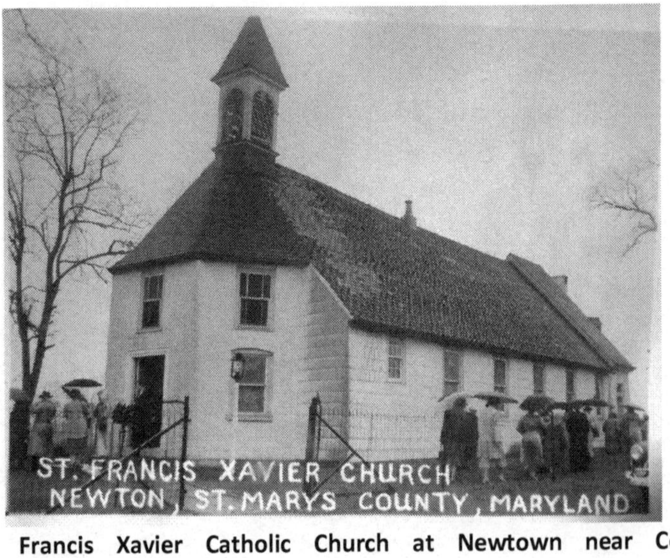

St. Francis Xavier Catholic Church at Newtown near Compton, Md.
From Mayor J. Harry Norris III Collection.

The Kalmar Nyckel on the Potomac River. *THE CHESAPEAKE photo*

CHAPTER 9 BAR DOG MANIA

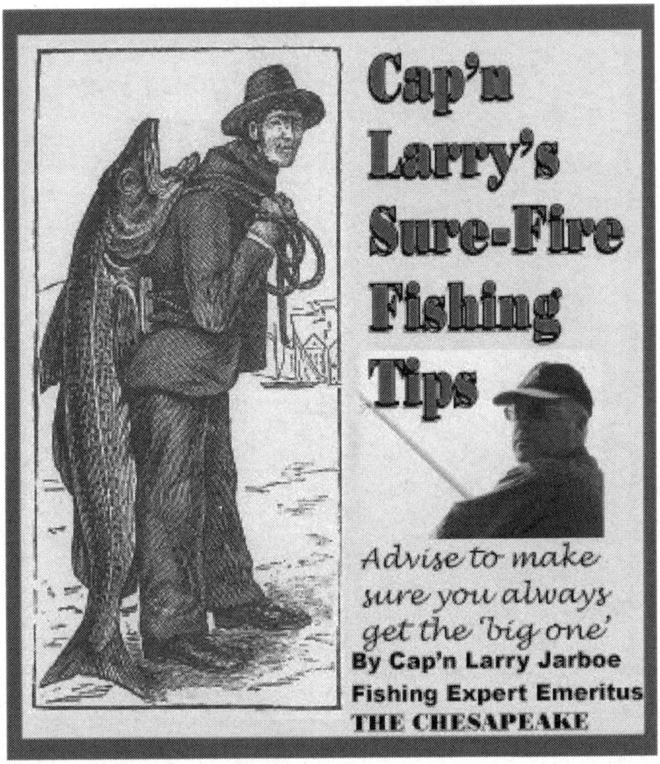

Cap'n Larry's Sure-Fire Fishing Tips
Advise to make sure you always get the 'big one'
By Cap'n Larry Jarboe
Fishing Expert Emeritus
THE CHESAPEAKE

The worst fish to catch in the Chesapeake Bay watershed has to be the Oyster Toadfish that is also called the Oyster Cracker or Bar Dog. If you have ever caught one of these fish, you remember what it looks like.

The Bar Dog is a slimy brown fish that has a big head with strong jaws. It has a small soft body with no scales. The Oyster Toadfish actually makes a catfish look pretty good in comparison. If Flip Wilson ever caught a Bar Dog, he would label it beyond ugly. "Fugly" was his word for such a visual obscenity.

I don't know if I would ever have written an article about Bar Dogs, but there are some very ominous signs heading this way regarding the upcoming 2011 fishing season. The weather so far has been pretty cold, damp, and nasty. I have heard of few good reports regarding local Yellow Perch or catfish catches. The early charter expeditions prior to the Trophy

Rock Season that begins on April 16 are sensing that most of the spawning Striped Bass have moved up the Bay.

Are Bar Dogs going to be the main catch this year?

While searching the Internet for Oyster Toad information, I found a fishermen's forum that discussed the edibility of the Bar Dog. Though I had never considered putting such an abomination through my lips, a poster named "Puppy Drum" claimed that Courtney's Restaurant in Ridge served fried toadfish appetizers.

Obviously, I made a trip South to visit Tommy and Julie Courtney to see if they served such a unique dish.

Julie Courtney said the fish they served was not toadfish but blowfish. This is the Northern Puffer which is also called Sea Squab. The Internet poster was wrong. I made a point to have a fried scallops basket while Tommy Courtney provided an excellent education about early Spring pound net fishing, the scarcity of herring, mud shad gizzards (which may be the heart), shad depletion in the Atlantic Ocean, and 15 inch rain events that make the blue-eyed Oyster Toads disappear. Tommy pretty much knows more than anyone about what is going on in the Lower Potomac. He is very concerned as well about the health of this year's fish, crab, and oyster fishery.

One thing that I have personally developed in my 58-year life span is a reputation for having Plan B ready to implement. Does Plan B mean Plan Bar Dog? If there are only Bar Dogs to catch this year, how in the heck do you cook them?

Some years ago, I collected a bucket of Oyster Toadfish to grind up for chum. The skulls loudly cracked like crushing rocks as they broke up in the screw and cutter head of my #32 Chop Rite electric chum grinder. The meat came out as clear gelatinous goop very much like the inside of a Spiny Lobster tail when you wring the tail from the body. Maybe, rolled and fried in cornmeal or beer batter, clear toadfish filets slid from that slick skin will taste like fried lobster.

Maybe not, that bucket of ground up Bar Dogs didn't make very good chum.

Still, this year, I am going to eat a Bar Dog or at least take a bite out of one. My departed fishing buddy Wayne Suite used to put every toadfish we caught on the bait board and drive a specially sharpened screwdriver through its head before releasing it overboard. One bite will tell me if I should sharpen my filet knife or my screwdriver.

Bar Dogs bite on pretty much any bait as long as it is near the bottom. Slack tide usually produces the most Oyster Toads as that is when most real fish stop biting. They put up virtually no fight at all. I will be interested if any of our readers has ever cooked and eaten a toadfish and survived to tell the story.

The Oyster Toadfish is a very tough critter that lives in polluted waters and even out of the water for a long time. NASA sent Bar Dogs into space to study the effects of micro-gravity on the development of otolithic organs (fish ears) and discovered the little difference. Maybe, this is one reason the space program is losing funding.

Let's hope the fishing is better this year than the indicators presently are showing. The times are tough enough without having to promote Toadfish Tournaments or Bar Dog Cooking Competitions. Get your boat and tackle ready, but pray we don't have to take Plan B.

No toadfish here! THE CHESAPEAKE photo by Capt. Steve Scala

Florida Keys fishing by Cap'n Larry Jarboe at the age of 23.

CHAPTER 10 ALMOST FREE DIVING

By Cap'n Larry Jarboe
The Chesapeake

How many loyal readers of the CHESAPEAKE remember watching the courageous exploits of Lloyd Bridges who played Mike Nelson in the T.V. series, "Sea Hunt"?

I sense this very fictitious but thrilling show spawned a generation of undersea adventurers who later adopted Jacques Cousteau as our more practical mentor.

One of the most differentiating realities between both Lloyd Bridges and Jacques Cousteau and us is the very expensive cost of scuba diving in exotic locations around the world. The men who swam with whales, fended off sharks, cut the exhaust hoses of foreign agents, and wrestled with that stuffed alligator could afford to jump into the water in the most exotic locales.

Their trips were paid for courtesy of the T.V. networks.

Unless you've got as good a gig as a movie star, you are going to have to pay your own way to experience the kind of undersea experiences we have all witnessed on television.

However, if you're willing to avoid the cost and hassle of scuba tanks, regulators, weight belts, and extensive certification process, you can enjoy the world of underwater wonder for the small investment of a mask, snorkel and fins. This sport is called snorkeling or free diving though there is a minimal cost for the gear.

The most important piece of equipment needed to view beneath the surface is obviously the face mask. Years ago, good masks were made of rubber with a tempered glass faceplate. Now, silicone rubber is the industry standard with two tempered glass lenses. The silicone seals out water well and lasts for many years.

If you have good eyesight, you can purchase your mask almost anywhere. However, if you are a first timer, drop by a local dive or water sports store and ask a knowledgeable staff person to help you select a reasonably priced, quality mask.

They should then show you how to put the mask to your face with the strap hanging loosely. Inhale trough your nose and the mask should stay in place with no leaks. If the mask does not stay in place or a steady stream of air flows in as you inhale, try on another mask. Stick with a simple mask that fits well.

For those of us who need corrective lenses, particularly for nearsightedness, a good dive shop will have lenses that you can try out to get as close to your prescription as practical before opting for a custom ground mask. Since water magnifies objects by twenty-five percent, the dive shop solution usually works fine. Though your choice of mask skirts may be limited, the ability to see is why you're buying the mask in the first place. You can make the fashion statement with your bathing suit (or lack of one).

Though you can see underwater with a dive mask, unless you invest in a snorkel, you will regularly have to lift your head above water to breathe. A snorkel turns a person into a porpoise by putting the breathing hole above the water behind your head.

My most sincere recommendation is to purchase the simplest solid snorkel you can find. Today, many snorkels have a valve below or beside the mouthpiece. In another article in this issue of the CHESAPEAKE, you can read about a friend of mine who nearly drowned due to this option. Stay with a solid tube of reasonable diameter and a comfortable mouthpiece. I still prefer the old J style tube which was invented by Captain Jean Jarboe when he had to hide from Piscataway Indians in the swampy waters of Jug Bay up the Patuxent River in 1638. But, that is another story. Also, the J-tube makes it easy to hang your mask/snorkel combo anywhere for quick access.

Attach your snorkel to your mask strap with a simple rubber or silicone snorkel keeper. My scuba dive instructor insisted that the snorkel hang from the right-hand side due to the placement of the scuba air supply hose. However, if you like the left side better, we still live in a free country.

Choosing a comfortable pair of fins may be the most difficult part of the three piece package. For most of us, a slip-on pair of fins that matches your shoe size is the best option. Make sure they fit snug but have no chafe points. Also, insist on a floating pair of fins. A fin that floats on the surface is a heck of a lot easier to find than one that sinks to the bottom.

Should you intend to do a lot of snorkeling in rocky beach areas, you might want to make a larger investment. You can buy coral shoes with a pair of adjustable strap fins to make your entry into the water as painless as possible. Talk to the dive shop staff about this combination if you intend to become a world traveled, seasoned snorkel diver who intends to explore reefs beside limestone or volcanic islands.

Finally, you should invest in a gear bag to keep your equipment together. This is probably the most personal choice you will make. Initially, use a small mesh bag that holds all of your snorkeling gear. Later as you decide to travel different places you can purchase a bigger bag to hold beach towels, a water bottle, and fruit or snacks or whatever else you might carry on day excursions. The small mesh bag will still come in handy as a compact carry-all folded in with your stuff.

With your gear assembled, you are ready to make your way to a swimming pool to get used to learning to snorkel and practicing in a calm, safe environment.

I will teach you how to use your new gear efficiently and look like a snorkeling pro anywhere in the world you might go.

Part Two

Last month, I shared the most affordable way to start diving without expensive and complicated equipment. Free diving which is also called snorkeling is easy to do for anyone who can swim. My four-year-old son, John actually learned to swim when he put a mask and snorkel on at the edge of a clear lagoon. While he was looking through the mask and breathing through the snorkel, he started to do the dog paddle around the shore. He is now thirty years old and a certified diver. Time sure does fly by.

If you missed the article last month about choosing your gear, you can go on-line at [the-chesapeake.com] to learn how to choose your gear. Last week, I visited with Mike Broomhall, who runs the Sea Dive Shop in Solomon's to get a local perspective on snorkeling. He is happy to help people choose good basic gear and offers courses in both snorkeling and scuba diving.

Most likely, you can teach yourself to snorkel if you choose good gear and find a nice warm indoor swimming pool to practice in while you are waiting for the weather to warm up. One of the most comfortable pools in St. Mary's County is at the Wellness and Aquatics Center at the College of Southern Maryland in Leonardtown.

There is one very important piece of gear to add to your mask, snorkel, and fins when you use a public pool. Make sure you grab a bottle of liquid spit from your local dive shop. Liquid spit is not really spit. It is defogging fluid. It is not a good idea to spit in your mask rub it around and rinse the nasty mix into a pool full of people. The ocean is a far more forgiving to use the natural expectorant process.

So, with your mask, snorkel, fins, and plastic bottle of liquid spit assembled at the edge of the pool, administer the defogging fluid to the inside of your mask and rinse according to directions on the container. Make sure your snorkel is hanging from your mask with the all-important snorkel keeper. Put on your mask and stick the mouthpiece of the snorkel in your mouth. Now, breathe nice and easy through your mouth as your nose is out of commission (like when you have a bad cold).

Ease into the water, stand on the bottom, and put your masked face into the water while mouth breathing through your snorkel. Your rate of breathing should not change. If you start to hyperventilate, lift up your head, calm down, and try again.

Once you feel comfortable looking around through the clear chlorinated water and breathing through the snorkel tube, you can swim on the surface. Initially, be sure not to submerge the open top of your snorkel underwater. You will find how easy it is to swim without holding your head above the water and how much fun it is to watch the other swimmers in the pool.

After you become accustomed to snorkeling and swimming on the surface, slip on your fins at the pool steps and practice kicking with your fins on. If you kick with your legs straight with a little flex at the knees, you will be amazed how well you can propel yourself with a pair of fins.

When you get used to swimming on the surface with your fins on, looking through your un-fogged mask, and breathing easily through your snorkel, you are ready to take your first trip beneath the surface.

Simply hold your breath, flip your feet up, and dive under the surface of the pool. The snorkel will fill with water, but you are holding your breath so the water stays out of your mouth. When you rise back to the surface, blow out the stale air you've been holding to clear the water out of the snorkel but save a bit. The first breath you inhale should be a cautious breath to make sure you have a clear tube. Should some water remain, hit a second quick exhale with the air you saved to fully clear the tube. Swim on the surface awhile and take another dive when ready.

Now, you know how to free dive.

In the years before my son or my daughter (Jodi learned to snorkel when she was three years old) put on their snorkeling gear, I taught over twenty thousand people to snorkel and visit the underwater world of our South Florida coral reef ecosystem. I never lost a customer. Hopefully, each of the students in my sea-going snorkel classes brought back an appreciation for the natural beauty of the world beneath the surface that most people will never get to witness.

Soon, I will share places in our Country you can take your gear to snorkel beyond the concrete pond at the community college.

Almost Free Diving - Part Three

If you are a regular reader of the CHESAPEAKE, you have learned over the past two months how to select and operate snorkeling equipment.

Clear shallow water generally is the prerequisite for an enjoyable snorkeling experience. Unfortunately, clear water on the mid-Atlantic coastal plain beyond indoor swimming pools is generally cold. Right now, the Bay and river waters are pretty clear and will stay that way through mid-May. If you have a thick full wet suit and are of hearty constitution, you can snorkel along the shoreline of the Chesapeake Bay and local rivers. Believe it or not, you can find fossil shark's teeth, giant prehistoric scallop shells, ancient whale bones, and other fossilized remains if you snorkel the cold clear waters in front of cliff formations.

A trip to the Calvert Marine Museum might whet your appetite for getting wet over the next couple months. Later on in the season, when the water warms, algae clouds the water and sea nettles move in. Both these conditions markedly diminish the snorkeling experience. Not seeing the bottom is bad enough. Not seeing that stinging jellyfish that you just swam into is enough to make you hang up your snorkeling equipment.

Sea nettles are not a problem in freshwater quarries. There are many former rock mining pits in Pennsylvania that have filled with water and are open to the public for warm season swimming. The water is still pretty cool but a swim top breaks the chill and you can witness bream along with largemouth and smallmouth bass in their natural freshwater habitat. Many years ago, I snorkeled in the cold clear waters of a Colorado creek. I saw big rainbow trout that took my breath away.

Actually, it was the temperature of the water that too my breath away.

The best, most diverse, and warmest snorkeling State in the United States is Florida.

The many snorkeling opportunities in the Sunshine State actually exceed the Caribbean Islands. Not, only does Florida have some of the most heavily fish populated offshore coral reefs anywhere in this hemisphere, the near-shore snorkeling is remarkable. Anywhere off the saltwater shore of South Florida, whether it is ocean or backcountry, clear shallow warm water may be found. Over the grass beds, rocky bottom or soft sandy bottom you will witness undersea natural beauty.

My first Florida snorkeling experience came when my Dad took my cousin and I down to Miami Beach for a couple days. I had been snorkeling off the beach and was asking a surfboard vendor about the bleached sand dollars he was selling. He said, "I saw you snorkeling off the beach. I could use some help collecting a new batch." So, he gave me a surfboard and a dive bag to use and we both headed for deeper water.

We arm paddled about a quarter mile offshore and slid off our boards into the ocean into about ten or twelve foot of water that had about thirty or forty foot of visibility. Much to my surprise there were dozens of live sand dollars scattered across the bottom. In less than a half hour, we both filled our bags and were stroking our surfboards back to shore.

As we hit the shore, my father was greatly relieved to see me. He had been running up and down the beach looking for me. I didn't tell him where I was going. Cousin Bobby said that I was swimming way out there past where I could be seen.

A couple years later, big George Henderson and I traveled south to Miami to escape the cold weather. We decided to go further south till we got to the Keys. We were amazed at the clear waters on either side of the bridges that connect the islands. We spent weeks exploring the clear waters right from shore and learning about the tropical paradise that we never knew existed.

Also in Florida, there are clear freshwater springs, lakes, and rivers. In these crystal waters, you can snorkel with freshwater fish, turtles, manatees, and other creatures.

One day while canoeing and snorkeling for fossils in the Peace River on the west coast of Florida, I spotted a hole under the bank of the freshwater river. I held my breath and swam into the cave to see what was inside. An alligator about five foot long swam out beside me. I made a subsurface beeline for the entrance and scrambled up the bank with my flippers slipping on the nearly vertical surface.

I spat out my snorkel and told my girlfriend who was sunning herself, "I just saw an alligator!"

She just shook her head. She always knew I was crazy.

Locally, I am not the only Southern Marylander, who has met an alligator in the Peace River. Mike Broomhall at the Sea Dive Shop in Solomon's has his own harrowing tale about coming nose to nose with a really big gator on the bottom of that Florida river. In his store, he also has a beautiful collection of fossil shark's teeth and other curios he has discovered while diving.

You can discover a whole new world of adventure just a few feet from shore by simply donning a mask, snorkel, and fins and slipping beneath the surface. Odds are you won't be facing sharks or alligators, but you will see real underwater life that most people never will witness. The price is reasonable and the payback in memories is priceless.

Austin Helton with a great catch!

A snorkeling family adventure.

Photo by Cap'n Larry Jarboe

The Bridgetender's office on the Pocomoke City Bridge at Pocomoke City, Md. After several reports to the town office one day were ignored, the bridge draw span section fell into the river. No one was on the bridge at the time.

THE CHESAPEAKE Photo by Ken Rossignol

The Bay Lady heads out of Crisfield harbor for a day of crabbing.

THE CHESAPEAKE Photo

PEPPER LANGLEY:

My boat building years and M. M. Davis Shipyards

"Nothing is more beautiful than a woman's bottom or the bottom of a boat"

Pepper Langley with one of his models. The Chesapeake photo

Dale & Cindy with great catch from Point No Point Lighthouse.
Photos courtesy of Buzz's Marina

Larry Jarboe exposes what your legislators have done to ruin the engines on your boat, in your lawn-mower and even your weedwhacker...

THE GRAND AMERICAN SCAM

Pepper Langley with a model boat that was in the works. This was a recent front page of the monthly edition of THE CHESAPEAKE

Classic sailing day on the Potomac as this sailing crew heads to the Chesapeake. THE CHESAPEAKE TODAY photo

A school of dolphins head into Breton Bay from the Potomac River in August of 2015. THE CHESAPEAKE TODAY photo

CHAPTER 11 **SOFT CRABS EARN TWO CENTS**

Growing up in Solomon's
By Pepper Langley

Well, here it goes:

I hate to do this to our young generation but rather than looking forward to going to the moon, I am looking backward to the cove where I was born, on the Back Creek in the upper part of Solomon's.

I will start back when I was quite a small boy. Like all of them, I was always getting into something --- some good and some bad.

Anyway, if it was good, I never heard about it, but if it were bad, I could not sit down very well for a few days.

One of the best times we had been the days when we would go crabbing for soft crabs in the summer months when the water was warm.

Because of our age, we were not allowed to use the rowboat until we were about 8 years old and the days when we were allowed to use the rowboat, it was like a modern day teenager getting a car.

No one will ever know what it is like to crab around the shores and beaches in your bare feet with the mud squeezing between your toes until you do it.

But don't try it now, there are too many glass bottles and beer cans and you may get hurt.

Everything we had to look for was bootleg whiskey bottles that washed over from St. Mary's and oyster shells, which we soon got us to.

There was nothing that looked any better to us than a large soft crab as it meant $.02 in our pocket if we sold it before it got too hard. If we caught 2 dozen, which was not too hard to do in those days, we knew we would go to a movie on Saturday night and have enough money left over for ice cream which we all liked.

As we got a little older, about 8 years old, we could get the rowboat, and then we could go fishing in the evening providing we got home before it got too dark.

We never had to worry about catching fish in the waters around Solomon's as there was plenty large hardhead (croakers), trout, white, perch and yellow perch, all the fish we wanted was a nice bite of soft crab bait, if it was on the old Norfolk fish hooks, you could catch all you wanted.

As we got older, we were out fishing at 4 a.m. when you could catch the most and largest trout.

When you got tired of catching fish and your fingers were cut from the old hand line, you would stop and come in to sell your fish.

Speaking of hand line, we never saw such a thing as a rod and reel in those days because they never even sold them in Solomon's until I was 12 years and in those days, it would take us a month to pay for one, but we liked the old line.

We used to use the white line with 2 hooks on it. These lines had a 6 oz. sinker on the bottom end and above the sinker was one hook about 12" from the sinker with about 8" of fishing line on each hook out from the main line. If you got your hook too close to the sinker or bottom, all you would catch were toadfish which no one would eat as we had plenty of good fish to eat.

One of our greatest ways to travel when I was a boy was a "ROWBOAT".

We almost lived in a rowboat.

If we needed ice, we would row to the ice house down in Solomon's to get it, if we needed groceries, we would row down to Webster's Store or Bafford's Store to get them. Also down on the Drum Point Farm, we would get chickens or corn to feed them when we were raising them.

It just seemed that everywhere we had to go, we had to row the boat to get there, same as getting milk and butter. We rowed across the back creek to get it from Mr. Hunkerford's farm and that had to be done before we went to school in the morning!

You know when I sit down and think of these days, I think if everyone had a good rowboat, they would not need all the barbells and other physical equipment that they buy today.

I can really say that you may not get muscle bound but it is good for legs, arms, back and chest muscles.

It never made me a prize fighter, but I never had to run from many fights except when I was losing and I sure knew when I was losing.

When we crabbed over on St. Mary's side, we had a small sail which we were sure would not turn the boat over and we would sail across and sail back as most of the time.

If the wind was blowing, it would be faster and we could get the crabs back to Solomon's before they would die. Most of the time when we were crabbing, we would put the Buster Crabs in a live box, but when they shedded we put them in wood buckets to fill out a little and then pack them in shallow wooden boxes, and put wet seaweed over them to keep them cool and out of the sun as the heat would kill them.

When we were crabbing for soft crabs, we did not bother to take any hard crabs as we had nowhere to keep them but to throw them in the bottom of the boat.

If they did not get a chance to bite your bare feet, they would die waiting to get their chance.

--- A Solomon's Boy Called "Pepper."

A carving for the old Lighthouse Inn created by Pepper Langley, left, is held aloft by the restaurant's late owner Richard Fischer. THE CHESAPEAKE photo by Ken Rossignol

This photo provided by Malcolm Morris identified the boy as himself and noted that he could get 5 cents for large crabs and 50 cents for a dozen soft crabs.

CHAPTER 12
BATHING SUITS NOW REQUIRED

By Cap'n Larry Jarboe
The Chesapeake

All of us who enjoy boating have our share of tales to tell about our own dumb conduct on the water. Sometimes, the story has a tragic ending from which we should all learn to avoid repeating. When the outcome is more humorous, those circumstances probably could never be duplicated nor would you attempt to. When you've been there once, you're not going back, not for the potential loss of life, but fear of further embarrassment.

My first job in the Keys was working as First Mate on the M.V. Discovery, which was a 124 passenger glass bottom boat working out of John Pennekamp Coral Reef State Park in Key Largo, Florida. This was a darned good job to secure. I felt fortunate because the stack of applicant papers was an inch thick. Later, the park concession manager confided to me that I was the only person who ever applied for a job there who was appropriately dressed to interview. I had spent my last few dollars for a baby blue polyester short sleeve shirt and a navy blue tie just for that day. Though I never wore that outfit again, it was a pretty good investment.

After my hire, a naval style khaki shirt and pants became the order of the day as my uniform on that boat. The daily routine was a great learning experience for me. I was fortunate to work with two experienced tonnage captains, Capt. John McGinnis and Capt. Clint Tyrell, who literally showed me the ropes to become a real mariner.

Initially, I lived at the Park docks on a 26-foot wooden sailboat built on Lake Erie that I traded my Ford van for on Marathon Key. This old boat was constructed in 1928. After living in a sailboat cabin with no standing headroom for six months, I purchased my own small house trailer on a rented lot. The seventy-five dollar monthly rent included water, sewer, and electricity. After selling the sailboat, I paid a hundred and fifty bucks for a powerboat that was on land. The owner threw in the trailer that needed a new axle. The original axle had disintegrated from salt corrosion.

Just a mile south from my single wide house trailer there was a famous welder named Barefoot Stanley, who welded while he was barefoot (hence the name) kicking hot molten slag aside as he worked. The Mother Earth News Magazine in her heyday did an article about Stanley's recycling efforts:

Stanley had been welding in Key Largo a very long time. When a new neighborhood was built beside his scrap pile, some of the ladies in the neighborhood association complained about the disheveled status of Stanley's property. The Monroe County Planning and Zoning inspector cited Stanley for his scrap pile. Rather than fight City Hall, Stanley simply welded the junk metal into works of art around the property depicting the snooty attitude of the people who were complaining against him. Barefoot Stanley became a world famous artist in at least one major magazine and the P&Z Department let him be as works of art are perfectly legal.

Barefoot Stanley must have seen me coming a mile away. He charged me seventy-five bucks for a very rusty, barely serviceable axle that he pulled out of his almost depleted scrap pile. When he had to cut off the springs, I witnessed first-hand how he got his name. I would have been screaming for mercy to have that much molten metal hit the tops and bottoms of my feet. Forking out a month's rent for a piece of art to bolt under my trailer was an equally painful blow to my limited budget but, with a homemade trailer hitch made out of pressure treated 2x6, I was able to get the boat into the water. I could not afford to purchase another metal sculpture (a used trailer hitch) from Stanley to bolt under my 1965 Mercury Montego Keys cruiser.

With my little 16 foot faded fiberglass boat of unknown make and an old 40 hp Johnson motor that started most times by itself and always with starting ether, I was ready to explore the many reefs and wrecks of the Upper Keys far beyond the itinerary of that big old slow glass bottom boat that was my daily bread and butter and ticket to a 100 ton master's license.

This is where the averted tragedy and actual comedy begins:

One day, after work, my buddy Dan LaCross dropped by the Park. Dan had abandoned his life in Michigan to bring his family to the year-round warmth of the Keys about the same time as I had. We had become true friends and fellow good pirates of perpetual plunder.

We decided to take a quick trip out to the first patch reef area called Mosquito Bank to hunt for new lobster holes and unfound Spanish treasure that we were always looking to uncover. After a short fifteen minute run in the 16-foot powerboat, I threw the anchor at the edge of Hawks Channel and the shallows of Mosquito Bank. This particular Danforth anchor was tied to an old polypropylene lobster trap line that Dan and I had picked up in the mangroves while beach scavenging. I really should have added a chain between the anchor and the line to help the anchor snag on the bottom, but my budget was busted from buying that overpriced axle from the barefoot buccaneer.

Neither one of us had brought our bathing suits, but we did have our gear bags. So, Dan stripped to the buff, put on his snorkeling equipment and bailed over the starboard side while I did the same over the port rail. Each of us went in separate directions as the buddy system does not apply in this particular situation unless, of course, you are snorkel diving in Key West which I have never done.

After a few uneventful minutes of exploring under coral heads and searching around big barrel sponges for spiny crawfish, I looked up to see my powerboat at least a hundred yards away sailing into the setting sun. Dan was unsuccessfully trying to catch the fleeing boat that was being carried down Hawks Channel by a 15-20 knot wind. Dan was a determined swimmer but not a fast one. His left leg had been crushed in a motorcycle accident a few years prior and he only swam with one fin on his good leg. As I watched, Dan turned from the departing power boat to swim for the fixed security of nearby Mosquito Bank reef tower light.

The severity of this situation quickly was imprinted on my total psyche as the adrenalin kicked in during my marathon swim to catch our escaping ride home. I was a pretty good swimmer but, this evening, I flew faster across the surface of Hawks Channel than Olympic swimming medal winner Mark Spitz could have ever clocked. As I steadily caught up with the speedy drifting boat, one thought flashed in my mind:

No way was I going to spend the night naked with my fellow nude buddy Dan sitting on the frame of Mosquito Light tower.

Inevitably, we would be picked up by the same glass bottom boat I should be working on during their early morning trip past Mosquito Bank light on the way to Molasses Reef. Such an outcome and the residual scuttlebutt would have been impossible to live with in the small town of Key Largo.

"Nope. That is NOT going to happen!" I thought as another surge of adrenalin kicked in pushing this St. Mary's County boy gone native to a new level of speed and endurance as my feet and arms pushed and pulled in smooth coordination.

About a half mile down Hawks Channel, I caught up with the end of the anchor line. The combination of a short scope of the line in the deeper channel water and lack of a chain encouraged the anchor that had pulled loose to skip across the grassy bottom rather than grab fast.

A few more quick power strokes and I swung myself over the stern using the outboard motor lower unit as a step. Thankfully, the outboard motor which was still warm started quickly without the ether assist. Dan was still struggling to make it to the light tower when I caught up with him and pulled him aboard.

He was nearly drowned and spent the next five minutes coughing up water and thanking God I had made it to him in time. His snorkel had developed a massive leak. Dan had been inhaling water with every breath and his snorkel would not clear with a sharp exhale.

After we had dressed back into our work clothes, we both inspected Dan's snorkel from the secure deck of the boat with the outboard quietly idling aft. The flap on the fancy (and, in my opinion, totally unnecessary) water relief valve beside the mouthpiece had folded in two during the stressful event making the snorkel a giant straw into the ocean. A minute more under these circumstances and the local newspapers would have had a true tragedy to report upon. And, I would have lost a very dear and wonderful friend.

That snorkel is probably still lying on the bottom of Hawk's Channel.

Key Largo days of Cap'n Larry.

A prize Snakehead fish. Photo courtesy of Buzz's Marina, Ridge, Md.

CHAPTER 13
SOMETIMES IT'S TIME FOR PLAN B
BY CAP'N LARRY JARBOE
THE CHESAPEAKE

The warm spell that we experienced last month in February almost convinced me to de-winterize my boat and head up to the warm water discharge canal at the Chalk Point Power Plant on the Patuxent River. The thought of cranking in a nice mess of ten-pound channel catfish nearly overcame the realization that I would have to re-winterize the boat when real winter returned. Instead of fishing during those balmy days, I prepped my boat, trailer, and truck for the day when I can launch my rig without fear of future freezing weather.

One of my projects during this spell is securing and mounting a "Plan B" motor for the inevitable day that the single inboard engine in my 20' Shamrock fails to allow me to return to the dock.

Plan B is usually not a problem with twin engine boats. In fact, other than increased docking maneuverability, the get home insurance of a second engine and running gear is the primary reason anyone would want twice the cost and maintenance of a single screw vessel.

Tow insurance is a good idea for the vast majority of us who have single engines in our boats. However, if you are twenty-five miles up the Patuxent River in January trucked deep in the Chalk Point discharge canal, it is going to take a while before your friendly towboat operator from Solomon's Island gets to you. Maybe, you should install a "Plan B" motor.

It does not take a huge outboard motor mounted on a "kicker bracket" to take you home at three or four knots. I used to run a 25 diesel powered 6-passenger fishing/dive boat from a campground in Key Largo. I mounted a spring loaded anodized aluminum marine outboard motor bracket on the port side of the dive ladder at the stern of the boat. In the forward cabin, I kept a 5 horsepower 1965 Evinrude Angler outboard that was stored upright clamped to another simple bracket. This kept the outboard from bouncing around and the float in the carburetor bowl from sticking. This is the fundamental reason to always store outboard engines upright. The plastic gas tank full of pre-mixed fuel was stored in the stern under the broad gunnel.

Twice, once on a fishing trip and once on a dive trip, I was able to use the outboard to take the boat home when a mechanical problem occurred that was not repairable at sea. In both events, we had a fine time putt-putting back to the dock telling boating adventures and fish stories. The divers even gave my mate and I a twenty dollar tip which is remarkable. Most divers, me included, are notoriously cheap.

A very reasonably priced means to make headway when the main engine or marine drive train fails are to use an electric trolling motor. Most well-equipped boats have a couple of heavy duty batteries that will power an electric trolling motor for a few hours. That should be enough to get you to a safe dock from most river and Bay locations. The electric trolling motor is a good affordable "Plan B" choice for trailerable boats in the range up to 20 feet.

In the Chesapeake Bay area, a marine rated trolling motor is the proper match for a smaller boat. Freshwater electric trolling motors are not designed to meet the corrosive rigors of saltwater immersion. During this cold spell transition to spring, I chose a Minn Kota Riptide 45 that was delivered new to my door for less than three hundred dollars. Before my first trip out this spring, it will be mounted and wired for use.

Not only will I have a cost effective "Plan B" motor to avoid the hassle and embarrassment of being towed home, but I will have a time-tested motor to try out some slow trolling techniques for white perch after limiting out on striped bass. In the past, I have paddled home with a tee shirt tied over a crab net or sailed in using my Bimini top. Though these are still options, they are relegated to "Plan C" and beyond. Now, I think a spinning prop connected to a working motor is the better idea.

You have numerous options to get your boat back to the dock when the power train fails. If you take a little time and investment installing a system that works for you, it can pay back big dividends in saved tow charges. Plus, it makes you look like a well prepared, smart boat operator. Someone might even call you Captain when you help them get back to the dock after a mechanical mishap. Please, stay safe and don't forget, "Plan B".

CHAPTER 14 THE OTHER MOOSE PIE

By Mark Robbins
THE CHESAPEAKE

Once upon a time eight moose hunters traveled across a mighty continent to hunt moose in the snow-covered wilds of Alaska. Upon arrival in Alaska, they were told that the cook they had engaged for the two-month hunt was ill and could not go with them. No other cook could be found. So the eight hunters drew lots to see which of the eight hunters would be the cook.

It was decided that the hunter that drew the white marble from the bag of marbles would be the cook for so long as no one complained about his cooking. It was agreed among all the hunters that the first hunter to complain about the cooking would become the cook. The marbles were drawn: the cook was selected and the eight men set off into the interior of Alaska to hunt moose.

Days and weeks passed, but all was not happy with the hunters. Although no one had complained about the cooking all were unhappy with the meals. They were never good. They were always bad, they always got worse, but still no one complained.

The cook, who felt cheated because all he did was cook, cooked worse meals every day. He did strange things to food. For breakfast, he did such things as serve scrambled eggs buried in grease and mixed with pounds of red hot peppers. Lunch was cold cod fish balls floating in cod liver oil. Every meal was worse than the last, but no matter how horrible he made the meals no one complained.

It seemed that the cook would never be able to hunt. Certainly he would never hunt if no one complains about his cooking. So in desperation the cook decided to serve the other seven hunters a cooked moose pie. He thought surely that they would not eat such a meal. No hunter wanted to hunt bad enough to eat a moose pie. Now the cook was happy he had found a way to hunt moose. Now all that remained was to find a moose pie, cook and serve it. He spent the afternoon before supper cleaning and polishing his hunting guns so sure was he that the very next day he would be hunting with the others and someone else would do the cooking.

Shortly before the seven hunters returned to camp for supper, the cook went forth and found a large, fresh moose pie which he carefully transported back to the camp. He wished to serve the moose pie intact so all would recognize it and complain and liberate him from the drudgery of daily cooking.

Finally, the moment arrived and the soon-to-be-liberated cook placed the large, cooked moose pie in the center of the round table where the hunters were all seated. There was silence and there were glances between hunters, but no one complained. So the cook cut the cooked moose pie into sections and offered the first section to the hunter he thought most likely to complain. He even asked this hunter to tell him what he thought of his new and unusual creation. The hunter so selected took the sections of moose pie offered him and did bite from it a large piece and chewed it. Then, without even changing the expression on his face, said to the cook, "It tastes like moose but good, but very good."

These piers were cut off from the shore at Solomon's by Hurricane Isabel in 2003. THE CHESAPEAKE photo

CHAPTER 15 WORKING AT THE TOMATO FACTORY IN SOLOMON'S

By Pepper Langley
The Solomon's Islander

When I was a young boy, the trustees of the Old Maryland National Bank, which I think was the Eastern Shore Trust Co. at the time, decided to build a Tomato Factory in Solomon's. It was located at the head of the back Creek, which today would be located behind the ACE Hardware in Solomon's.

As far as I can remember the Tomato Factory was built around 1925 to 1927 and at that time was doing very good.

The farmers just above Solomon's Island that were also in the business had large fields that grew very good tomatoes.

But this was a seasonable crop and had to be harvested in just a short period of time and in that short time they had to have as many workers both in the fields and in the factory as they could get in order to get the tomatoes canned before they got too ripe or they could not be used.

That is where all of us young boys come in.

If you were strong enough to lift a bushel of tomatoes, you could get a job and most boys at the age of 12 years could lift a bushel of tomatoes.

When I was 14 years old, I got a job picking tomatoes in the field. That is where you had to start and there were no labor laws at that time as many boys and girls were working at home in the tobacco fields when they were 8 and 9 years old as the family had to make a living and it was seasonal also.

Most of the days we picked tomatoes it was sweltering.

Bending your back most of the day would be very tiresome and the most tomatoes we could pick were about 4 bushels a day.

You did not pick long in the evening as the tomatoes would have to set over until the next morning to be steamed and they would be no good to can.

After we had picked our 4 bushels of tomatoes, we would have to lift them on the wagon which was horse powered. We would be given brake tokens that had a hole in the top of them and we would put them on a wire clip and keep them until we wanted to turn them in on Friday to get our money which would be at the most $1.00 a day as we received 25 cents per bushel, but that was good money in those days if the weather was good and we could pick.

After you had done a good job in the fields picking, some of us got jobs working on the wagons and from there working in the factory putting the tomatoes on the water belt.

They would go through a steam process and come out where the women would skin them and put them in the cans from there they would go again through a steam cooker and come out to be capped and then on to the room where they would get the labels stuck on and packed in boxes to be shipped to Baltimore, most of the time by large schooners and motor buy boats.

Even when we were kids at work, we would always take time to have a little fun and when there were no bosses in the field where you were working and no one watching, you would be looking down picking tomatoes and would feel one bounce off your head.

The first thing you would do is look up and guess who was the one that did it and then you would catch him with his head down and return the good deed to square with him.

Then you come to find out you squared with the wrong person so that started a real battle.

After the boys were splashed from head to foot with tomatoes they would soon calm down and go home smelling like a rotten tomato but being boys that was all included with the day's work and they still had plenty of tomatoes to can.

Pepper Langley with one of his carvings.
THE CHESAPEAKE photo by Ken Rossignol

CHAPTER 16 A BOOM TOWN GROWS UP

By Ken Rossignol
THE CHESAPEAKE

LEXINGTON PARK (June 1990) --- Failing to fold up its tents and steal away into the night as if a group of camel herders, Lexington Park has become one of Southern Maryland's most vibrant and influential communities. The dire predictors of the base closing that were forecast by jealous folks in Leonardtown worried about their loss of control of life in St. Mary's County, never came to fruition.

Over the past forty years since Lexington Park was written about in the old Washington Star, the orderly boom town described in 1950 has perhaps become a little disorderly in ways, but has certainly continued to boom.

The housing area described has become one of the area's lowest cost housing while expansive and expensive residential developments from condos to luxurious million dollar waterfront homes provide shelter for a much larger collection of people. From aircraft mechanics to school teachers, test pilots to convenience, over 35,000 people now reside within 15 minutes of the main gate of Patuxent River Naval Air Station.

The remote Southern Maryland town that in 1950 was known for its trailer homes is amazingly enough now becoming a bedroom community for the Washington, D.C. area.

When folks were hollering for a four-lane highway to be built from Pax River to Washington, perhaps they never realized that people would use it to commute to work while sleeping in St. Mary's.

Along with the expansion of residential areas have come the construction of four major shopping centers in the Lexington Park area, that now includes California.

The former bump in the road known as California used to consist of Millison's Store and Post Office, Norris's Store and Dexter's. Now, the area boasts a four-lane highway, Larry Millison's new show piece, Sans Souci Plaza, the Wildewood Shopping Center and several smaller strip centers such as Laurel Glen, Hickory Hills and the now aging Esperanza Shopping Center.

The Naval Air Station has expanded with all manner of testing of aircraft and weaponry systems. The Naval air patrol of the mid-Atlantic region remains a station purpose and the Test Pilot School is a major tenant on the base. Other groups such as the Naval Air Logistics Command and the Naval Mess School bring great diversity to this area.

With the expansion of the testing, duties have come the growth of Defense Contractors. Particularly in the 1980's, the large buildup of the Reagan Administration made massive changes to the landscape.

For the first time, off base, office space became a significant factor in the local economy. Huge buildings have sprouted up, some on the town's main drags of Great Mills Rd. and Rt. 235 and some tucked away to spots like Wildewood and at the South Gate of the base.

The first really beautiful apartment complex in town was built in the 60's. Queen Anne Apartments by Harry Waller and since then numerous projects have gone up that cater to the decidedly upwardly mobile middle class that holds the military, civil service, and contractor jobs.

Five elementary schools, two middle schools, and a high school serve the Lexington Park area in addition to the private and parochial schools.

The first shopkeeper of Lexington Park was Hiram Millison. He was booted off the base as the navy rushed to construct the Naval Air Station when World War II broke out. Millison ran a general store in the community of Pearson and while he may have been out of a store he was not out of foresight. He acquired the land located at the main gate.

Hiram Millison worked day and night alongside his workmen to construct a restaurant, bus station and eventually shops that would have a grocery, drug store, and countless services that catered to the needs first of the workmen constructing the base and then the military personnel that staffed it.

Being hardworking and understanding what his customers wanted ran in Hiram Millison's family. His father Israel Millison, known everywhere as "Jake," came to America shortly before the turn of the century from Lithuania. A significant part of this nation left Europe in those days to escape the endless wars and to seek the freedom and prosperity of the United States. Jake Millison spent two years on a doggedly determined quest winding his way through Europe to arrive at a seaport and make passage to Baltimore.

Jake managed to buy out a peddler that worked as a type of traveling branch of the Epstein Department Store in Baltimore and that's how he landed in St. Mary's County. He found his sweetheart from Lithuania in Baltimore and he and Sarah settled in St. Mary's County.

Jake's son Hiram built up a typical general store and the rest is history. Hiram Millison became an important part of the St. Mary's Community. St. Mary's has an unusually high number of business people that take an active role in the affairs of the community and the Millison's are no exception. When one enters the St. Mary's County Courthouse, you see Hiram Millison's name on the dedication plaque as a member of the building committee and in the Leonard Hall Governmental Center, Larry Millison's name is listed on that plaque.

Slot machines have been gone for over 20 years from St. Mary's County but a curious change has occurred. The State government has started running both numbers and a lottery, every day and perfectly legal! It seems when talking to many local people that the day of slots will be seen again.

While there have been many people central to the development of Lexington Park since 1950, Maryland Bank & Trust President Jack Daugherty and Developer Larry Millison have been the key players.

Millison says of Daugherty, "No one has helped people get the money they need for a car, a home or to start their business like Jack has." Of Millison, Daugherty said, "Larry Millison invests not only his money in his hometown but he has put his heart into it as well."

Larry Millison served one term on the Board of Education and three terms as a County Commissioner. Expressing a conservative/populist political philosophy, Millison has gained support from broad segments of the County's population. Independent and determined, Millison has always cherished the late St. Mary's County Circuit Court Judge Phillip B. Dorsey and the legendary and still active Senator Paul Bailey. Even today Millison is considered a possible candidate for St. Mary's County Commissioner President and remains as unpredictable as ever. Many folks that supported Larry over the years have found him on the side of the taxpayer and the infamous 'little people'.

To imagine a stooped over small man named Jake carrying a 300-pound pouch on his back, trudging up a dusty road from the steamboat wharf, then you understand what Larry Millison remembers and knows his roots.

In another forty years, it will be the pleasure of another writer to update the history of this small town, and while it may not be small, it will most likely have an entrepreneur named Millison planning a structure and renting to people with the aspiration of achieving the never-ending American Dream.

(Since the publication of this article in 1990, St. Mary's County has continued to boom; Larry Millison died in 1998 and Jack Daugherty in 2000. Millison Development continues to be operated by Rachelle Millison, who operates retail centers and office complexes.)

This was Great Mills Road in the 1920's when wheelbarrows were given as much space on the highway for cars.

Photo courtesy of Malcolm Morris.

Larry and Betty Millison present a check for Navy Relief and the Annual Air Expo at Pax River NAS from them and the Belvedere Motor Inn. THE CHESAPEAKE photo

Vote the WINNING TICKET in St. Mary's County
PRIMARY ELECTION - MAY 20, 1958
TAWES
For GOVERNOR
MAHONEY
For U. S. SENATOR
DORSEY
For STATE SENATOR

The Dorsey campaign ticket in 1958 when Jack Daugherty ran against Dorsey in the Democratic Primary. Dorsey won.

St. Mary's Commissioner Eddie Bailey, Del. John Slade, St. Mary's States Attorney Walter B. Dorsey, Seafarer's School Director Col. Ken Conklin at the Seafarers Neighborhood Watch kickoff in 1991. THE CHESAPEAKE photo

Larry Millison was labeled 'the Jewish cowboy' by a Baltimore Sun writer. Millison had several large farms in Maryland and Florida. Raising cattle and speculating in racehorses' sometimes kept his business afloat when he experienced losses in real estate.

Larry Millison at the site of the construction of his Millison Plaza at the main gate of Pax River NAS in Lexington Park, Md. Photo courtesy of the Baltimore Sun.

CHAPTER 17 **WILDCATS WITH WHISKERS!**

Catch cats year round with no limit in Patuxent south of Rt. 214 Bridge

By Cap'n Larry Jarboe
THE CHESAPEAKE

BENEDICT --- One of the most cooperative fish to catch that swims in tributaries of the Chesapeake Bay is the catfish. The Patuxent River divides Calvert County from Charles and St. Mary's Counties. From Golden Beach cruising north past the Chalk Point power plant, there is some very fine fishing to be had for tidal catfish.

The two primary species usually caught are the channel catfish and the native white catfish. Small channel cats are a bronze olive color with distinctive small black spots on the sides. Larger channel cats over five or six pounds often become more bluish gray in color though the spots remain. The white catfish is the native catfish in the Chesapeake watershed. White catfish are smaller fish. They seldom exceed six pounds. The white catfish is dark blue with a marble white belly. They have a much larger head than the more sleek channel cats. The white catfish, according to my taste, is a much finer fish to eat though proper preparation makes both species provide a fine meal.

Catching these good eating fish is easy. The season on them is open year round. There is no limit in the tidal waters below the Rt. 214 Bridge. The size limit is 10 inches, but let those little ones go as there are plenty of big ones waiting to grab your bait.

Good bait is the key to catching a big mess of channel catfish. Right now, local seafood dealers like Thompsons Seafood in Mechanicsville save scarce herring and common mud shad for anglers to use for bait. Herring is the best cut bait but mud shad soaked in menhaden oil is pretty good, too.

Till the end of April, soft shell clams a.k.a. manoes are a darned good catfish bait. Also, fresh peeled shrimp cut into a plug that will not spin in the current are fine bait. Keep those manoes and fresh shrimp on ice through the trip. If the fishing isn't so good, you can eat your bait.

Shore fishing involves rigging up a surf rod with around twenty-pound test line. The traditional double hook bottom rig with 2/0 or 3/0 hooks works very well to present a couple different baits to check for the cats dining preference of the day. I like to also rig another rod with a sliding egg sinker on the main line tied to a swivel, 4' leader, and single 5/0 hook embedded through the lips of a herring or spot head and trailing entrails for the bigger cats. When that big cat bumps the bait, you can drop the bail and feed a few feet of line freely through the sinker prior to setting the hook. Then hang on.

It will take a little scouting to find a good spot along the shore around Benedict and up the river. Much of the access is private property so permission is necessary. There is a nice public community park just north of Eagle Harbor where I have watched anglers catch good stringers of fish. A little scouting ahead of time is a good idea.

If you are fortunate to have a boat, the DNR launch ramp on the Calvert County side of Rt. 231 will put you close to the heart of Pax River catfish country. The Chalk Point outfall canal just south of Eagle Harbor is one of the finest places to fill up a cooler of catfish. The same rigs and bait should be used, but shorter rods equipped with spinning or bait-casting reels are a better tackle.

I have had good luck in different parts of the power plant channel depending upon the season. The water is slightly warmer most times of the year and too hot in July, August, and most of September.

Watch your fish recorder for single large fish near the bottom to mid-depth. Those are most likely catfish. I've yet to see a fish finder that shows whiskers. Find an area where they show most frequently and anchor up current.

One of my tricks prior to leaving the dock is to mix up a mess of thawed chum and clam or oyster shells in a bucket. After the boat has settled on the anchor, I take a big ladle and chuck large globs of shell and chum mix behind the boat. The commotion that sounds like breaking fish and the chum stuck to oyster shells pretty much guarantees the cats will be beating a path to the bottom acreage behind your stern.

Next, methodically put out a spread of four or five rods with a smorgasbord of baits spread from one side of the creek to the other. It won't be long before a rod tip starts twitching. Let the fish take the bait deep before setting the hook. If you would like to find some of the menhaden oil I mentioned earlier to spice up your bait, readers of the CHESAPEAKE are welcome to call my number on the front page. A free sample of the stinky stuff is my gift to the serious catfisherman or woman.

This year in the peaceful waters of the Chalk Point outfall canal, I caught seven nice channel cats on New Year's Day in a couple hours to celebrate my separation from my past job. Two weeks later, I came back and caught seven bigger channel cats some of which topped ten pounds.

Now that this long cold winter is behind us, there are big fish that we can catch prior to the trophy striped bass season that opens up April 17. Next week I plan to make another trip up the Patuxent in my 20 Shamrock to stock up on a nice mess of catfish filets for the smoker.

I hope to see you there.

Cap'n Larry Jarboe with a big bunch of catfish.

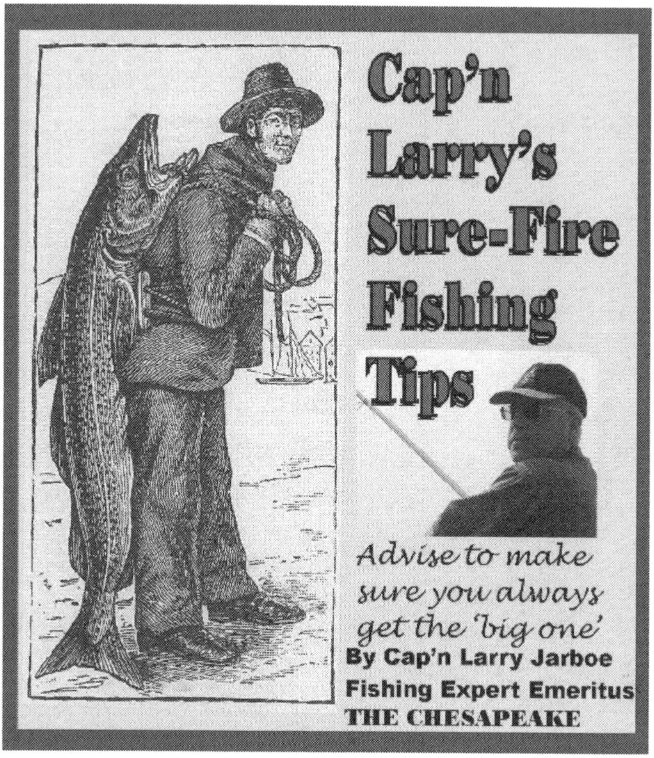
Cap'n
Larry's
Sure-Fire
Fishing
Tips
Advise to make
sure you always
get the 'big one'
By Cap'n Larry Jarboe
Fishing Expert Emeritus
THE CHESAPEAKE

CHAPTER 18 **STINK BAIT**

By Cap'n Larry Jarboe
The Chesapeake

Carl Stewart was one of my favorite fishing buddies who has moved on to that great fishing hole in the sky. He was my father-in-law as well. I thought his daughter also harbored the same passion for fishing, but it only lasted till we got married. That is another story.

Sometime in the mid-80's, Carl drove from Springfield, Ohio to our home in Patuxent Knolls for a visit and vacation. It was early spring about this time of year. I had just launched my 25' KenCraft that I kept at the community dock in Golden Beach.

We decided to run up the river on Easter Sunday as most everybody should be in church and we would have the whole Chalk Point power plant canal for our own private use.

The day before, we had gone to Paulie Thompson's fish house to pick up some herring for bait. There were no herring left. I noticed that high up in the fish case were three black mullet. I had never seen a fresh black mullet in Maryland, but I knew the fish catching potential of these oily bait fish. So, I was happy to purchase all three mullet.

Upon arriving home, I cut the mullet into bait strips. Put the strips in a quart jar. Poured menhaden oil inside. And, placed the capped mix in the fridge.

On Easter morn, Carl and I took our rods, cooler, and chilled congealed stink bait to the boat and headed upriver. When we got to the discharge channel of the power plant, there were at least a dozen other boats who had also figured the same strategy.

Humbly, we eased into the swarm and anchored trying to keep a respectful distance from the multitude of fishing neighbors who had also avoided Easter service. We baited up four rods with the pungent slick baits and cast out around the boat.

There was an ultra-light rod of mine that had a very short handle. It was equipped with a small Gold Penn spinning reel. I asked Carl to place it in the flush mount rod holder carefully as it could easily pop out. A few minutes later, the rod flew out of the holder and into the water as the first catfish struck.

Carl felt pretty bad, but I learned a good, albeit expensive, lesson about stubby rod handles. Neither one of us had much time to mourn the lost rig as the cats started biting like crazy.

Out of the three rods left, one rod was always occupied with a fish on. Most times, we were both cranking in catfish. No one on any of the other boats had caught a fish and we were throwing catfish in the cooler by the dozen.

About a half hour into the feeding frenzy, Carl had a fish on amidships in the stern. I had just hooked a channel cat on the port side and the starboard rod bent over hard. I reached across and set the hook. Now, I had a rod in each hand on either side of the boat and no hand free to crank.

Undaunted, I alternately stuck the handle of each reel in my mouth and cranked a few turns by spinning my head. When both fish had come to the surface beside the boat, I made a sweeping fluid motion with the two rods and dropped both fish simultaneously into the cooler.

One of the nearby skiffs then putt-putted over. The fisherman said to us, "I've been watching you guys catch fish for the past half hour and none of us have gotten a bite. That last move was the last straw. What are you using for bait?"

I told him, "I'm going to tell you, but you will not believe me. We are using cut black mullet soaked in menhaden oil."

I might have just as well said that we were using pickled squid lips. He looked at me, sniffed the smelly jar, and motored away shaking his head.

Sometimes, the truth stinks.

CHAPTER 19 **FROM PILOT TO INNKEEPER**

My First 30 Days Out of the Navy

By Jack Rue
The Chesapeake

(Editor's Note: Jack Rue has been a longtime resident of St. Mary's County. We asked him to tell us how the beginnings of Lexington Park as the business hub of the county took form.)

I had the good fortune to fly six congressmen around the world, heading west. It is claimed that this was a first as it was against the prevailing winds. When I received orders, I was unsure about whether I should go regular Navy, go back to Ann Arbor and get my law degree or simply to hang my hat here.

My wife Penny and I went to see Mr. W. J. MacNeil, assistant sectary of the Navy, and two congressmen. They suggested that I ship over and continue to fly VIP's. I told Mr. MacNeil, known affectionately as Mr. Mac that we were considering opening a business in Lexington Park. MacNeil noted that Patuxent River was going to be one of the largest naval air stations in the world because of its proximity to Washington, D.C. He also said that the runways over the water, the availability of 7,000 acres and the air space reserved for testing were all positive indications of continued growth.

He also said he wanted to come down and see us and asked me to show him the base. He came down on a Sunday and said he wanted to see the base anonymously. There was a picnic going on at the Officers'

Club and we walked around. Admiral Shouffle was there and I introduced him. On Monday morning, the admiral called me and nicely advised me to notify him when I had distinguished visitors. I told him I'd comply the next time I brought Winston Churchill.

I had not seen Cadet (Jack) Daugherty since our Pensacola, Fla. Days. Penny and I went to the club about August 1945. There were a big band and Capt. and Mrs. Daugherty were jitterbugging. They had a large crowd watching them and I hollered, “Hey Dog, you dance better than you fly.” That is where it all started.

He had bought an acre outside the gate where Raley's Furniture Store is, saying he was going to open a gas station. I said I had been to Hi Millison and that I wanted to open a clothing store. He asked if I had ever run a clothing store before and I said, “No.” Then he said, “Every time I see you, you are sitting on a bar stool. Get behind the bar where the cash register is and get some of your money back.”

I responded, “Fearless Leader, that is the best advise that one pilot can give to another.” The reason he and Gabe Gabrelcik are well-to-do now and I am a pauper is they were selling gas by the gallon and I was selling booze by the ounce. I could also drink my product and they couldn't.

Daugherty introduced me to Phillip E. Grey and we signed a lease, which occurred in the spring of '46. The county was wide open, all types of gambling everywhere.

I went to see C. B. (Dick) Greenwell, Clerk of the Court and got my liquor license. He asked me only one question: “Are you a citizen of the United States?” I replied, “I did not buy these medals, wings and uniform at a pawn shop.”

Then I asked if I should go to the liquor board and the health department. He said, “We have none.” When I asked about Sunday sales, he replied, “I drink Saturday afternoons and Sundays and don't refuse to sell me a drink.”

I wondered about slot machines, and again he said, “We have none.” They were illegal at the time. You paid $50 annual tax to the federal government. Slots were on all the naval bases --- they were legal on federal property.

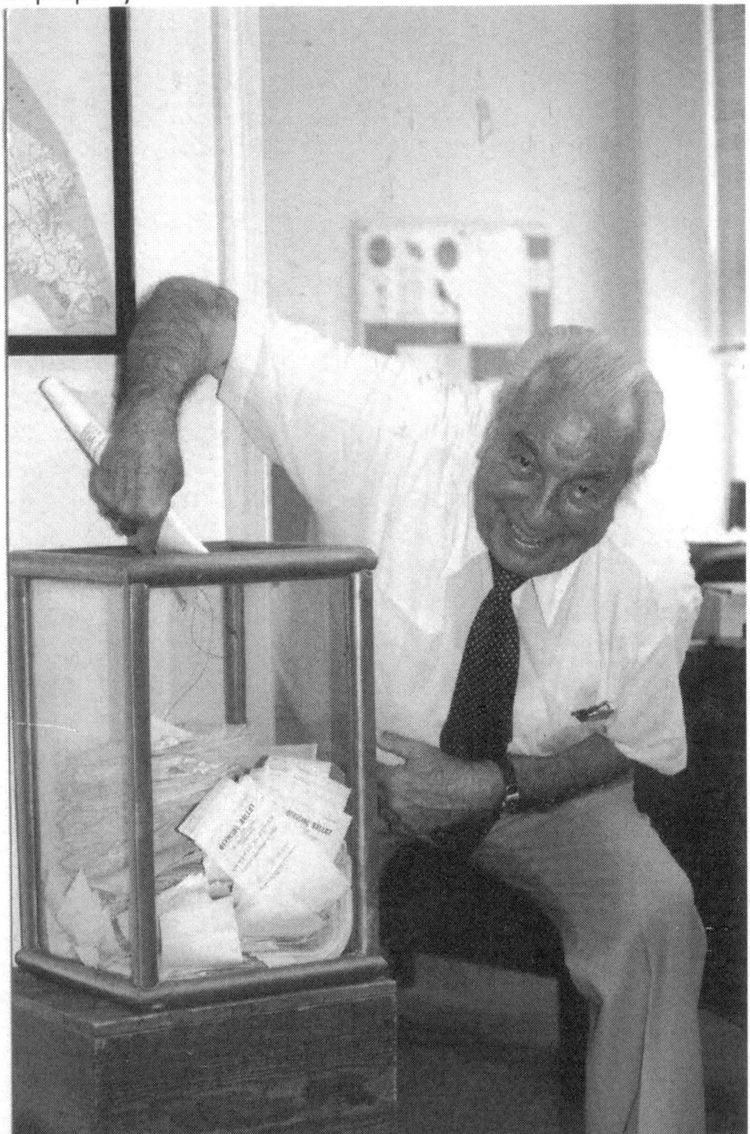

Jack Rue stuffs the ballot box. Rue ran for County Commissioner President in 1994 and in a debate repeatedly held up a "Wrong Way" sign as he made his point that his opponent, Barbara Thompson, favored raising taxes. THE CHESAPEAKE photo

My brother Medric had just gotten out of the Navy as a cadet, and he came to help us. Ken asked me to write 'My First Month Out of the Navy'. Being in transports, my flying was similar to the airlines --- only 80 hours a month with there's off the time off (except when I had line duty.)

Penny, Med and I spent our time restoring Batty's Purchase and the two tenant houses for rentals. The "Rue Purchase Road" was a logging trail; we borrowed a truck and the county loaded gravel from the Hayden Farm, which Jim Dobry bought later. Chap Thompson was head of county and state roads. The shovel was at the pit. I saw Hayden and asked how much a load. He said, "Fifty centers." I asked who was going to count the loads, to which he replied, "You are." Oh, for the good old days!

After we had bought Batty's Purchase, I went to the county commissioners --- J. Frank Raley Sr., Frank Bailey, and Matt Bailey --- and asked them to take the road over. When I left, Eddie O'Brien (no relation to the present O'Brien's --- unless you go back to Ireland) came in and they said, "Who does that lieutenant think he is? We have natives who have been waiting 40 years for us to take over their roads." O'Brien said I was not a bad guy.

He had the best club in the county. It was called Esperanza and it sat at the end of Green Holly Road where John Lore built his home. The clubhouse had a successful fire (how do you start a flood?).

We spent the summer of '46 getting supplies for "Rue's Roost," buying some new furniture from Woodies and getting wagon wheels from the 7th District.

My Navy friends named the place; they kept asking when "Rue's Roost" was going to open. The old one was where Raley's Furniture store is and we had a locker club upstairs for the enlisted men as they were not allowed to wear "civvies" aboard the base.

When you go to the new Roost, you will see the same bar, wagon wheels, etc. Mr. Page built both bars, and they got the brick for the fireplace from the old slave quarters at Tudor Hall --- so they say.

Charlie Himmelheber built the new Roost, and Jackson Raley built it. We opened the old Roost on Good Friday, 1947. I called three of my skippers, and they put this in the plan of the day for a week. "Jack Rue, one of our plane commanders, is opening a bar this Friday at 1800 --- all hands turn out."

It was payday; I thought the Navy marched out. There were very few cars and civilian clothes in 1946. Rationing was still on. The old Roost was supposed to be a hardware store, I am still biting nails.

The "know-it-alls" said we would go broke because we had tablecloths. You could not get near the place on Friday or Saturday. George Aud came in Sunday. I did not know him. He said, "Where are your name brands of booze?" We had none. He went to his liquor store and brought me two cases of assorted booze --- VO, scotch, etc. When I asked him how much I owed him, he said that salesmen would be here the next week to sell me all the right brands, adding, "This is a beautiful place, keep it that way." I said "Aye, aye, sir!" Where do you find a friend like that?

We opened the present Roost (now the Lexington) on September 15, 1950. It was another Friday --- payday --- and we did not close the doors until about 3 am on Monday. Johnny Dolak, Jack Daugherty, Bill Chapman, Harry Buckley and I carried the bar top down the street from the old to the new Roost --- cobwebs and all. I called it atmosphere.

We put beer on ice in garbage cans, booze and paper cups on boards, and the customers helped themselves. "Rue's Roost" never closed! All our help pitched in on the move. Fran Harris came with us on the Friday morning of the opening.

People ask me why I sold the place. "The booze got stronger, my wife nervouser and the girls faster." Any other questions?

St. Mary's County Md., Circuit Court Judge Philip H. Dorsey, bottom left, with his political allies. District Court Judge William O.E. Sterling is at lower right.

Kayakers are as common on the Chesapeake and tributaries as speedboats. THE CHESAPEAKE TODAY photo

The light atop the Blackiston Lighthouse on St. Clement's Island, recently rebuilt as a labor of love by volunteers. THE CHESAPEAKE TODAY photo

CHAPTER 20
ST. GEORGE'S ISLAND SHOWS NEW SIGNS OF SLIPPAGE FROM MAINLAND; INDIANS SET TO TURN IT INTO CASINO

By George W. Turlington
The Chesapeake

ST. GEORGE ISLAND, Md. (SPECIAL) --- A severe disturbance in the Gregorian Fault which lies underneath the Potomac River and affects an island attached to the mainland of St. Mary's County only by a bridge is once again showing signs of shifting.

Not since 1989 when the island actually broke loose from the mainland, causing the island to lose its Post Office and the road link to the Piney Point area has such an extreme danger to everyday lives of residents come into question.

A county commissioner, Francis Russell, lives on the island and has been bombarded with phone calls from his neighbors who are asking what the government is going to do to keep the earthquake-like event from severing their land connection with the mainland.

St. George's Island dangles by a threat to the mainland.

THE CHESAPEAKE photo

State Highway Administration trucks have set up a checkpoint on the mainland just before the bridge and have seismic monitors drilled into the ground at the bridge to monitor each and every tremble.

"We will shut this bridge down at the first sign of new cracks," said SHA spokesperson Judy Landau. "We cannot allow anyone to be endangered by being on the bridge at the time of gaseous trembling emitting from the deep recesses of the Gregorian Fault, which caused the bridge to be severed back in 1989. Engineers had provided the structural repairs necessary to the island with 742 metal rods which had been drilled into the northern end of the island to permanently anchor it to the south end of the bridge and we are doing Satellite surveillance of all of the changes in the positioning of the island over the past 12 months. At the first sign of movement, the bridge will be closed to traffic and after that residents are on their own for transportation to the mainland as the State of Maryland is already facing a $2 billion deficit. "Commissioner Russell vowed to conduct County Commissioner meetings on the island as a way of forcing the State of Maryland to provide ferry boat service. Commissioner Kenneth R. Dement told a resident of the island that "I'm not taking any boat to the island, I don't go on boats."

The popular Bull Wade, who has been the county executive for five terms, first elected in 1990, reported to the commissioners at last week's meeting that he had met with Congressman Steny Hoyer who said he was going to have the Department of the Interior study the suitability of the island simply becoming a national park and having each resident be given an I.O.U for their property, as the national government is already facing $14 trillion in debt and won't have any money to pay residents for their homes, but Hoyer reports that the SEIU has sent a proposal to the Obama Administration to give the island to the Mattaponi Indian Tribe who will then turn St. George Island into a casino.

"The Mattaponi Indian Casino will be able to provide car ferries to patrons of the casino, which will also include new high-rise hotels," said Hoyer in a statement delivered on the House floor a few minutes after the contentious health care issued was passed.

"It's a shame that someone didn't think of this sooner," said Russell. "Most of the people on the island are getting old and going to die anyway, so it's imperative that government act to prevent a new generation of aging Americans from moving in, growing old and then dying, the cemeteries are full and neither the county or the state government can afford to pay for ferry service, but the Indian Casino will be able to do the service, provide jobs and a strong source of tax revenue for county and state government, everyone wins under this proposal."

With the Mattaponi Indian tribe signing a 99-year affiliation with the SEIU last year, the two entities will work together to quickly move all of the St. George Island residents into FEMA trailers which have been brought in from a large FEMA storage lot in Purvis, Miss.

"This is a win-win, those St. George Island residents who would lost their homes due to the island separating from the mainland will be able to frolic in the lush pastures and woodlands of the nearby Take It Easy Ranch," said Russell. "They will be on high ground, not be a target for every north-Easter and hurricane, and for the life of me, I can't figure out why anyone ever wanted to live on the island."

The chief snag to the deal for the island is coming from the Seafarer's Union, which had been negotiating with the Mattaponi Indians to sell their Harry Lundeberg School of Seamanship facility at Piney Point to the Indians.

The two 6-story resort hotels already built at the Seafarer's school campus, along with dining and marina facilities would allow the tribe to quickly implement the license for slot machines it won last month from the State of Maryland as well as exercise its rights under an agreement with the Federal Government to settle outstanding litigation over confiscation of Indian lands in St. Mary's City.

"We have been promised a lot over the past couple of years," said SEIU President Fibing B. Eig. "We worked hard to get this administration elected and our members need jobs, we need to compensate the Indians for their native lands and someone has to pay for car ferries, so here we are, in the Majority Leader's home district to replace a bridge that will soon lead to nowhere."

THE VANISHING ISLAND FOLLOWS THE VANISHING WATERMEN – David Sayre points to the mainland from St. George Island. ***THE CHESAPEAKE Photo***

CHAPTER 21 **SKILLS OF A FARM BOY**

By Stephen Gore Uhler
The Chesapeake

I was trying to tie up a sack of sheep feed when I realized that the bag was just too full to get the string on. Rather than remove some of the feed, I got bull-headed. I pinched and squinched on the sack until finally I had barely enough material to get my string around. I took a few wraps and then realized that I had so much string I couldn't get a knot tied.

I nodded to my grandson.

"Cut off some of that string, Boy."

"Huh?

"Cut the damn string boy, my fingers are getting tired."

"With what?"

"With your pocket knife, son."

"I don't have a knife."

"You don't have a knife?"

I let the 100 lbs. of feed run all over the barn floor and dragged the kid out to my truck for a trip to the hardware store.

It just shows you how ignorant grandparents can be. I didn't know the boy was running around at 8 years of age without a pocketknife.

My grandson was sure tickled with his new knife, scarlet red plastic handle with a half dozen blades and even 2 corkscrews.

I don't know the reason for the corkscrew; I haven't seen a corked bottle in years except for that bottle of imported olive oil that was so rancid I couldn't use it, but anyway, the boy liked it. Everybody was happy, except his mother. You never heard such screaming.

"Where did he get this knife?"

"I bought it for him."

"You idiot!"

My daughter addresses me in such endearing terms. I think she learned them from her mother.

"I don't want him to have a knife. Suppose he would take it to school?"

"I certainly expect he would take it to school. How else could he sharpen his pencil, or carve willow whistles, or carve his girl's name in a beech tree? How could he join his playmates in a game of Mumbly Peg at recess without a jackknife?"

"Oh Daddy, you're such a relic. Don't you know that if he ever took this thing to school, the sheriff department would surround the school with SWAT teams."

Times sure have changed. An 8-year old boy in the good old days would rather go to school without his pants than without his pocket knife.

We used to take our guns to school back in the good old days. Not actually on the school property, but right up to the edge.

We would cut through the woods and squirrel hunt as long as we could and then at the first bell we would hang our game on a tree branch and stash the gun where we could resume the hunt as soon as school let out.

Those old Stevens single barrels could be broken into three parts with just a flick of the wrist, lock, stock, and barrel.

You could put each piece in a different tree hollow to prevent anyone from finding your entire weapon. I usually didn't have to take my shotgun apart; it fell apart every time I fired it. The lock was so worn that it would fly off every time it fired. I had tar taped the lock to the barrel but after several rewinding of the tape it would be so contaminated with sweat and gun oil that it wouldn't hold at all.

Such inconveniences only added to the challenge of the hunt. You knew you had one chance to bag your game and then find and reassemble your gun for another try.

That discipline as a child served me well later during my military service.

All my buddies wondered how I could report to the firing range and immediately qualify as an expert with every type of weapon.

It was easy. The sights weren't all bent up, the lock didn't fall apart. Qualifying was easy with those nice Government Issue weapons.

One feature of my old single barrel really helped me when I got into aerial gunnery. Most student gunners had difficulty hitting moving targets, but to me it just came naturally. The firing pin on my old single barrel was so worn and bent up from years of use that on really cold days, it would hang up and fire seconds after the trigger was pulled.

You couldn't put the bead on a rabbit, quail or squirrel and just assume you had him. You had to judge how cold the air was and how fast the game was running or flying, and point to the spot where you thought the game would be at the time that the firing pin decided to release. Tricky business that the hunters senses to perfection with each 12-gauge shell, costing 12 cents apiece; you couldn't afford to miss too many times.

We, boys, wanted to get a reloader so that we could make shells for less at 1 cent a piece but after Tommy Shields had burned his eyebrows off while reloading shells, Mama vetoed the idea.

Old time people believed in passing down, which simply means that the first born son gets anything he wants while his younger brothers suffer in jealousy.

My oldest brother got to use daddy's double barrel Ithaca that I wasn't even allowed to touch. It really made me mad.

George Hopkins penned this cartoon making fun of politicians and their sole qualification for office: BS. Hopkins signed his toons "Hop".

That gun ruined my brother as a hunter. The quality of his gun, along with the fact that he could get off two shots to my one led him to believe that he didn't have to practice his stalking skills. He thought that with that big double barrel with the gleaming barrels and shiny burled walnut stock that he could merely point it down through the woods, give 'em both barrels and pick up the game that fell at his feet. We would have had a bare cupboard if that boy had to keep it filled.

He looked so cute with his double barrels, his little red cap and leather hip boots with the knife sheath sewn in the top. The height of fashion, and couldn't hit a bull in the ass with a bass fiddle.

You would think that such treatment would leave me jealous, so blind me with rage that I would be less of a hunter.

But no, adversity is the best teacher. I would take my rusty old Stevens with the busted forelock, snow sticking to my unhatted head, dried holly leaves clinging to my unshod feet, a-hunting I would go.

One day it was blowing a blue gale, Mama was rooting through the pantry, trying to decide on a hot supper for such a cold, blustery day.

"A squirrel pie would go good today."

"Aw Mama, you know there ain't no squirrels out today, be a waste of time to go out."

The thought of one of Mama's squirrel pies with potatoes and onions with a thick brown crust sounded pretty good to me.

"I'll go out Mama."

"Son, why don't you let Stevie take the brand new double barrel with the shiny walnut stock?"

"No Mama, I'd feel better with my rusty old Stevens with the busted lock and bent firing pin. It's what I'm used to."

So I shouldered my trusty shotgun and gathering the thin cotton jumper across my chest, I set out into the teeth of the gale.

Squirrels don't usually come out in windy weather and the few that do venture out are hard to find, but this day was different, but for some reason the woods were full of squirrels.

I used the last strip of tar tape to wrap my gun together and prayed, "Old Betsy don't fail me today."

In a short time, I was back on the woodpile unloading my bag of game. I had squirrels in all pockets, squirrels across my shoulders and was dragging about a dozen on a string of barbed wire I had twisted off of old man Johnson's fence.

Mama had a whole nest of tinned baking pans, the biggest one was more than 2 feet square, and would just barely fit in the oven. We only used it during butchering time and referred to it as the "hog-killing" pan.

When my younger brothers and sisters peeped out of the kitchen door and saw the big pile of squirrels I was skinning, they hollered to Mama, "You better take down the "hog-killing pan". I was as proud of that squirrel pie as Tiny Tim was of his Christmas goose.

You didn't have to stir around amongst the potatoes and crust and wonder what kind of pie you were eating. It was squirrel pie. Big chunks of squirrel. The hot brown crust was not flat, it was pyramid shaped to allow for all the squirrel piled inside.

I would like to have saved that old single barrel but as WWII was going on at the time and metal was scarce; my brother cut it up to make tobacco spears.

The fancy double-barreled Ithaca came to a sad end also.

We had a game warden back in the good old days that would arrest his grandmother. You could be sneaking through the woods not making a sound and feel a tap on the shoulder. Warden Bill Cosden was not human, he moved through the woods like a spirit; and as I said, would arrest his grandmother.

We boys didn't pay much attention to hunting season; we figured it would be time enough to season the game after it was on the stove.

My brother had spotted Warden Cosden before Cosden spotted him, flipped his game bag one way and his fancy double-barrel the other and kept whistling down the path.

"Howdy do Mr. Cosden, nice day, nice day."

Mr. Cosden agreed it was a nice day and, of course, wondered what my brother had done with his bag and shotgun, but what the hell, you can't catch them all.

We boys went back and searched and searched for the discarded shotgun. We beat that thicket bare but could never find it.

I outwardly sympathized with my brother about the loss of his fancy shotgun but secretly I was about to bust with laughter. I was hoping that some way he would also lose his fancy hunting boots with the knife sheath on the side and his big red cap with the stupid looking ear flaps.

A fancy dressed dandy, no hunting would be complete.

Oh boy! Never did find that shotgun.

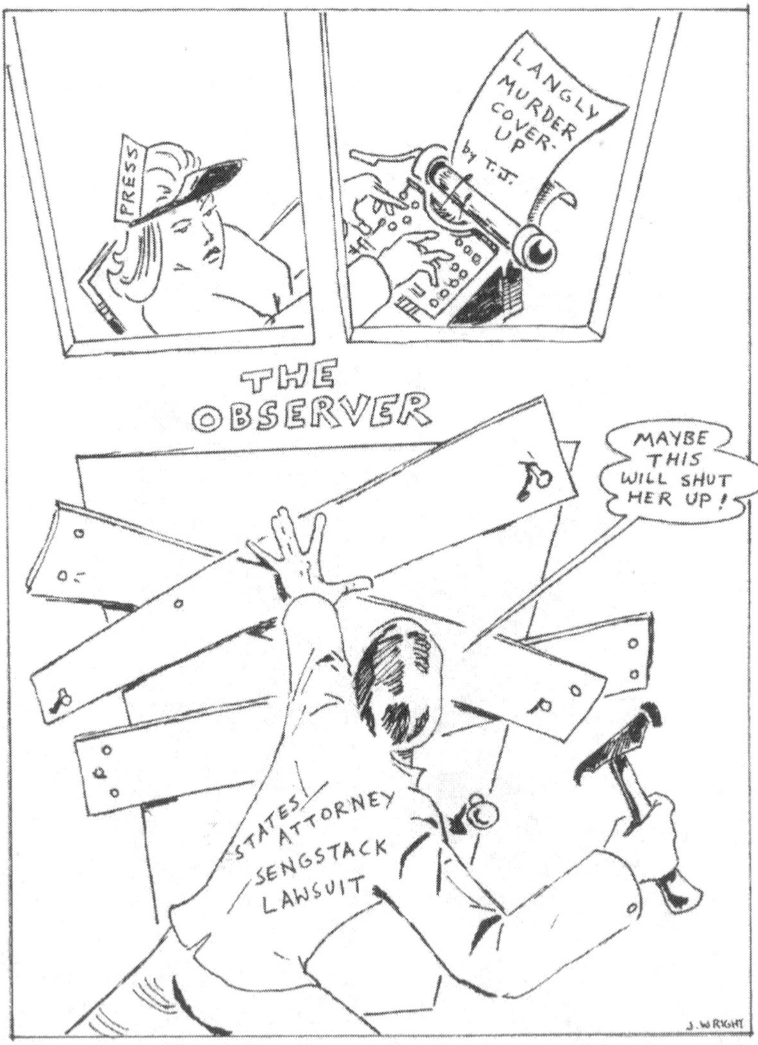

TJ DuCellier operated the Chesapeake Observer in Calvert County and battled with local officials over the Kevin Langley murder cover-up as shown in this cartoon which appeared in The Chesapeake and drawn by John C. Wright.

CHAPTER 22 **TEN YELLOW NEDS OR A COOLER FULL OF CATS**

By Cap'n Larry Jarboe
The Chesapeake

Fifty years ago, Allen's Fresh Bridge on Rt. 234 was the place to be during the first week of March. I remember well as a boy seeing anglers standing along the concrete railings with long stringers of big Yellow Perch. I looked forward to getting big enough to drive there myself and join the fun. However, by the time I got to be of driving age, the perch runs had diminished considerably.

As teenagers, during the peak of Yellow Ned season, Barry Roache and I launched an oak sided, plywood bottom prow that I built to fish ponds and creeks. Barry called my custom built vessel, "the Floating Hog Trough". We could slide it into the back of our family '56 Chevy station wagon and with a 5 horsepower Evinrude motor; it took us where we wanted to go beyond the shoreline.

On our only trip up Allen's Fresh during early March in the Floating Hog Trough, we caught a single Yellow Perch on the minnows we brought for bait. We thought we held the advantage with our boat over the shore fishermen who had hoofed their way up the muddy trail along the creek. Few of them were catching any fish either, but one guy positioned at a choice spot in the bend up the creek was catching Yellow Perch on a regular basis.

So, we tied the boat to a sapling on shore and moved onto the wooded bank to watch this successful fisherman from a respectful distance. The experienced fisherman was kind enough to take us into his confidence about his location as well as his choice of bait.

"Boys, the Yaller Neds like to rest up a bit in this calm deep hole here at the bend before they have to fight their way over the shallows to spawn up in the Zekiah Swamp." the Old Timer told us.

"Also," he continued, "Everyone else here is using minnies for bait. Minnies work all right when the fish are thick, but when they're scattered like today, a grass shrimp will catch 'em when the minnies won't buy a bite." He opened up his cool cup of sawdust mixed with a few small grass shrimp to show us.

The Old Man imparted wisdom that no fishery scientist is even aware of: "Y'all see, boys, that grass shrimp is a threat to the eggs of those perch. They'll bite that little bugger just to kill it."

Who knows if that old codger was telling the truth, but he sure did have a nice stringer of fish.

With the former scarcity of Yellow Perch and the very low five fish limit in past years, I have preferred to fish for catfish in March while waiting for the waters to warm and other fish start to feed.

The most common catfish caught in the Upper Patuxent and Potomac River is the Channel Catfish. The White Catfish is the native species found in the Chesapeake Bay watershed. I find that the White Catfish, which has a larger head and less forked tail is a better tasting fish, but with proper preparation, any catfish can be made delicious.

Catfish can be caught year round with no creel limit and a ten-inch minimum length. Bottom rigs baited with cut herring, spot, mud shad, fresh shrimp, soft shell clams (manoes) or soft crab will produce good catfish catches.

A couple weeks ago, while cleaning out the garage, I found an old log book with my fishing catches in spring during the mid-1980's. The average daily catch was about three dozen catfish that averaged about 2-3 pounds each. Now, I'll catch far fewer but the average weight is 8-10 pounds each. Things are always changing in nature which makes fishing so interesting and challenging.

Perhaps the most difficult catfish quarry is the monster Blue Catfish that have taken up residence at and above Mattawoman Creek in the Potomac River. A Google search of [Potomac Blue Catfish] will reveal fifty

pound plus catfish in our backyard waters that will bite on a year-round basis. These fish are caught using whole herring baits or live sunfish. I look forward to embarking on a monster cat expedition in March and writing about it in a future edition of THE CHESAPEAKE.

So, until the waters warm and the Striped Bass become legal recreational fare in mid-April, the basic March options boil down to an increased limit of ten Yellow Perch or a mess of big catfish. Why not do both?

Bushwood Wharf on the Wicomico. THE CHESAPEAKE photo

Quade's Store draws big crowds for downhome cooking and boating events at Bushwood Wharf located on the Wicomico River on the western shore. THE CHESAPEAKE TODAY photo

These two U. S. Army LCM's were hauling down the Potomac rafted together. The soldiers missed a great chance to waterski. THE CHESAPEAKE TODAY photo

CHAPTER 23
SNORKEL-FISHING: A CLOSE ENCOUNTER

By Cap'n Larry Jarboe

THE CHESAPEAKE

During a visit to Serges Performance Cycles Shop in Lexington Park, I spotted a very unique heavy duty beach bike outfitted with a small single cylinder engine.

"Looks like this is the DWI Transportation Special," I said.

Serge smiled and replied, "Yes, I need to hook up the clutch. There are a few engineering challenges that I have to overcome yet."

We had a nice conversation about motorized and electric bikes. Serge is a very smart guy. He will get his invention working before long.

I promised him that I would write a column in the November edition of the CHESAPEAKE about a sport that I invented and came to realize that, in the ocean, we are not top of the food chain.

There is a fish called the Hog Snapper or Hogfish that is found from the Carolinas down through the Caribbean. The Hog Snapper is not a snapper at all. It is a wrasse. It is not easily caught by hook and line because it generally eats crustaceans or mollusks. Most fishermen down South do not use crustaceans like crab or lobster for bait. Clams are seldom found as bait in South Florida either. Also, the Hogfish is a very picky eater. Despite the funny looking snout that is the mouth of older specimens, Hog Snappers nibble very gently, shying away from the imbedded hook. If they feel any resistance at all, the wary Hogfish will drop the bait and swim away.

However smart they are with hook and line fishermen, they are equally dumb confronting spear fishermen. These slow moving fish turn their broad bodies full side view to predators. It may make a grouper decide to find a smaller meal to swallow, but the spear fisherman gets a bigger target. Spear fishermen account for the majority of fat, tasty Hog Snappers harvested.

Over thirty years ago, the largest populations of Hog Snappers in the United States were found off Key Largo. This was the one area along the East Coast that was illegal to spear fish due to its special status as both a State and Federal Marine Sanctuary. Most fishermen could not hook a Hog Snapper and fishing with a spear gun was and still is illegal.

Three decades ago, I caught a crab from under a rock while exploring a patch reef behind the snorkel boat that I worked as a mate on. Any Maryland boy knows how to handle a crab. With the back paddler joint pinched between my thumb and forefinger, I carried it back to Capt. Dennis and formulated a plan:

We took the boat Penn spinning rod and reel combo out of the foc'sle. I broke the crab in half and hooked it on a 5/0 hook through the side joints. Then he left the bail open as I jumped back in with my snorkel gear and swam behind the boat looking for a fat, sassy Hogfish.

Sure enough, a big old hog was cruising through the sea fans and sea whips. I dropped the baited hook in front of him and swam back but still within watching distance. Then, like a musical director with my hands above water, I showed Capt. Dennis how to give the fish plenty of slack line. When the Hogfish passed the crab past its tender lips and swallowed the bait deep within its crushing throat, I motioned for Dennis to set the hook.

As the hook sunk in, the Hog Snapper threw the broad sides of its body in gear and swam back and forth wrapping the line around soft corals as it pulled the drag out. Once it stopped under a coral head, I simply snorkeled down, unwrapped the line from the Gorgonians (another term for soft coral) and pulled the fish out of its coral lair. Capt. Dennis cranked the hog back to the boat.

Each one of us got a big filet for dinner.

The whole routine of coordinating two fishermen, though successful, could be eliminated if the snorkeler handled the rod and reel in the water I surmised as Capt. Dennis and I discussed how to put a steady supply of fried or baked Hogfish on our dinner tables. Thus, the sport of snorkel fishing was born.

I bought a Zebco 404 spin cast combo, greased the internal gears with heavy marine lube, and loaded the reel with twenty-pound test line. Capt. Dennis purchased the same rig. He generally did not like to fish, but this routine was to his liking.

We took turns during our trips doing lifeguard duty while the other of us would seek out Hogfish with our snorkel fishing rigs.

Imagine if you will, the joy of seeing your prey and actually catching and fighting your fish in the clear warm Florida subtropical waters. We mostly caught Hogfish, though Dennis or I would settle for a Margate, porgy, or grouper if the hogs were scarce on a particular day.

We even had capturing bait down to an art form. We tossed the filleted carcasses behind our dive boat in the marina. Small blue crabs would feed on the remains and are found in the rocks behind the dive platform. As the first mate, one of my duties became diving behind the boat prior to a trip to grab a few crabs for bait.

We never got skunked in our snorkel fishing efforts. The general procedure was to get all our customers into the water. Then, Dennis or I would do lifeguard duty while the other prowled the grass flats and patches off the main reef for Hog Snappers.

Upon seeing a likely candidate for the cooler, we would cast to the fish and let the hooked bait settle to the bottom. Invariably, the hog would ease over to the hooked crab and gingerly pull on the bait. The key to success was to keep a slack line until the fish got the hook deep into the crushing jaws beyond the lips then pick up the slack and set the hook.

Then, the fish would take off making the drag scream on the little plastic reels. After dragging the line around as many soft corals as possible, the hooked Hogfish would settle under a coral head. The snorkel fisherman then simply had to wind the line away from the sea fans and sea whips and dive down to pull on the heavier leader line to withdraw the worn out hog from its hole. There was always a steady thump, thump, thump as the fish was extracted.

Pretty much we had become the master predators of our undersea universe until one day I noticed that George, the resident shark on Grecian Rocks, was taking a close watch over our delightful sport.

George was either a Dusky or a Reef Shark, who was almost six feet long. He kept coming closer as we were fishing but did not express real interest in the process.

Then, one morning when I hooked a hog over the undersea grass flats, George rushed in and tried to eat it as the Hogfish scooted under a coral head. George moved up from the brain coral with his mouth gaping right behind the fin of a snorkeler on the surface. I nearly swallowed my own snorkel when I witnessed the potential horror. Abruptly, George turned and swam toward me. Apparently, he knew the real culprit who was usurping his domain.

I had already broken off the line. The hooked hog was of little concern at that point. George circled me all the way back to the boat a rod's length away the entire time.

"Dennis, this shark is onto us. I'm not going snorkel fishing here anymore. Something bad is going to happen if we do this again." I told Capt. Dennis.

Well, that deal lasted for a week. Capt. Dennis informed me he wanted a hog for supper. I told him that I would not fish, but I would run interference for him. We had a second mate on board that day who was doing lifeguard duty. Dennis hooked a small hogfish that he pulled out of a coral head. The thump, thump, thump sounded like a dinner bell to me. I knew George was going to show up. Worse than that, the hogfish was gill hooked and trailing blood. Dennis broke off the leader and handed me the rod as he dragged the fish back to the boat.

I was behind Dennis in the blood trail when I saw George charging through the clear blue water in the distance. This time, he was shaking with his jaws snapping. I used the little spin cast rod to poke him in the nose to fend him off. I was actually getting pretty good at swimming backward and fencing with this very agitated shark when a smaller shark swam past my arm and joined in the commotion. Shorty, the other resident shark, which was only about three and a half feet long, joined George in a two fish tag team.

This stranger of the deep was photographed by Cap'n Larry Jarboe.

I was not about to be tagged it by being bit.

Capt. Dennis made it up the dive ladder as I porpoised right up onto the dive platform. We decided that day not to snorkel fish on Grecian Rocks again.

This should have been the end of the story, but snorkel fishing is an addiction not easily withdrawn.

A couple weeks later, I decided to try snorkel fishing one more time off of White Banks which is a patch reef far from Grecian Rocks. Other than an occasional nurse shark, I had never seen a shark around this particular area. The water was very green that day with only fifteen feet of visibility. Far behind the boat, I hooked a nice five pound Hogfish. With the hog subdued and gripped by the eye sockets, I was ready to swim back to the boat.

At the edge of visibility, I spotted the distinct black and white vertical pattern of a pilot fish. Never, have I seen a pilot fish swim alone. They always accompany a bigger companion, generally a shark.

I have only seen one Bull Shark in the water in my lifetime and I witnessed it that day. With the big Hog Snapper in my hand, I saw a ten foot long, big thick Bull Shark ease into visual range which was only fifteen feet away. This is the kind of shark that not only will bite you. A fish that big can tear your torso in two.

Instinctively, I dropped the fish which slowly swam to the bottom. I hoped the shark would take more interest in that stunned fish than the shocked fisherman who was smoothly swimming back to the boat. Not once did I look back through the murky water though I did pray to God the entire time. There would be no stopping a fish that big if it was determined to feed upon your carcass.

I made it back to the boat with my body intact and a story to tell. That was the last time I went snorkel fishing.

Diving for lobsters at Key Largo, Florida. Cap'n Larry, at left.

A traditional Chesapeake Bay crabber leaves the dock at Crisfield, Md.
THE CHESAPEAKE TODAY photo

CHAPTER 24 **STEAMBOAT DAYS**
LETTER FROM ST. GABRIEL'S MANOR

By Frederick L. McCoy
The Chesapeake

One summer when I was about fourteen, my mother arranged a steamboat trip on *The Dorchester* that plied the waters of the Potomac River and the Chesapeake Bay between Washington and Baltimore. One evening about five pm in August, we boarded our steamer at the 7th Street Wharf in Washington.

I was given a little stateroom and my mother and sister had another.

We had a number of passengers, some just for a summer trip, others destined for the various lower Potomac wharfs.

After taking on freight for different points, we took in our lines and the paddle wheel began to churn as we backed away from the pier and made our turn to go down the Washington Channel.

The pure white Norfolk boat *The Southland* was still at her dock as was the excursion steamer the Charles McAllister. We were soon past Haines Point and traveling south down the river.

At Alexandria, we stopped for a few minutes. A bit of freight and some passengers were loaded and off we were again.

It was time for supper and a Negro with a bell walked the ship announcing "time to eat." In the dining room were long tables with white cloths and silver.

The meal was served family style. Bowls of new potatoes, lima beans, and sliced tomatoes, ears of sweet corn and platters of fried chicken were in front of us.

The food was fresh, directly from the farm and it was cooked to perfection. While dining we heard the Dorchester give three long blasts on her fog horn and bell ringing for an extended period. We all knew that this was the customary procedure as a ship passed Mount Vernon where the Father of our Country is buried.

By the time, supper was over the sun had set and the stars and moon were rising.

We found deck chairs on the bow and watched the water separate and pass down each side of the steamboat until the great paddle wheels grabbed the wash and sent it hurling past our stern.

There are not many of us left who remember the old steamboats. I'm one of the fortunate and I find it hard to describe the times.

The dining room of the Southland steamboat.

Photos courtesy of Malcolm Morris and Fred McCoy.

The little wharfs were often set back well in some tidewater creek or bay and the boats were the main contact with the outer world. They brought Washington and Baltimore to the neighborhood. Everything came or went by the steamboat.

Sometime that night when were asleep in our bunks, I heard a commotion and found that we were about to tie up at a wharf. It was Colonial Beach. The gangplank was noisily slid to the wharf and farmer's freight destined for the commission men in Baltimore was loaded. A cull cow or two came on board and the howling of several veal calves must have awakened most of the passengers.

The livestock and produced was soon on board and we were again underway.

It was light when we made our next stop. It was Lancaster at Rock Point. I quickly dressed and was on deck before we had finished unloading ashore the freight that originated in Washington.

This wharf was in Charles County, Md. in tobacco country and several hogsheads of tobacco were rolled up the gangplank by the Negro roustabouts.

We crossed the mouth of the Wicomico River to St. Mary's County and put in at the Chaptico Wharf. It was time for breakfast and again we dined well.

There were pitchers of milk with pieces of ice floating in them. There as hot oatmeal and cream of wheat. There were fried and scrambled eggs, fried country ham, and country fried potatoes and biscuits. We all ate heartily.

At Bushwood Wharf, we were in a good seafood area.

The cook went out on the pier to see what several boys had caught that morning. He bought some strings of Norfolk Spot fish and some soft crabs. I wonder now if these boys were members of the "dirty dozen" who lived in the area. The children of the farms would bring vegetables from their gardens. The cook would look them over on the wharfs and only purchase the freshest and best. We would be eating the bounty of the tidewater from both the land and the sea at our next meal; all caught or picked that very morning.

Our old paddle wheel steamer, *Dorchester,* next turned into St. Clements Bay and stopped well up at Bayside Wharf.

Men dumping crabs into the cooker at Rock Point on the Wicomico. Photo by Theodor Horydczak.

Steamboat docks at Broom's Wharf at St. Mary's City. Photo courtesy of Cue Ball Raley.

John B. Abell had returned to the family farm and wharf after a stretch of being a commission merchant in Washington.

Here, case after case of mason jars were trundled off by the roustabouts and before we left a messenger from Guy's Store in Clements hurried aboard to give the purser an order for more jars and sugar to be loaded in Baltimore to be delivered when the *Dorchester* returned on her next trip.

It seemed that the farm wives were doing more canning than usual that year.

Some said that their husbands had also found a use of mason jars. Remember, those were prohibition days!

We crossed to St. Clements, stopped at Coburn's Wharf and off-loaded more jars and took on some hogsheads of tobacco. These hogsheads averaged about 750 pounds but could be easily rolled up the gangplank. The cask was made of native wood; several wires were wrapped around the outside and holding the head in, was a large wild grapevine nailed through the top of the sides. This held the pressed tobacco securely in the cask.

Down St. Clement's Bay, we churned and made a turn into Breton Bay. Our first stop was Abell's Wharf and then Leonardtown. Several ox carts had come down the hill to deliver this and that to the boat and soon Model T. Ford truck were used and freight to Baltimore was trundled aboard.

Here at Leonardtown, the county seat of St. Mary's County, certain traditions were upheld.

On the hill above the wharf at Tudor Hall, lived Colonel Swann, and an elderly gentleman who usually met each boat. He was seen coming slowly down the steep hill using his cane. He was dressed in summer white and wore a large southern type hat, a southern gentleman of the old school. He saluted Captain Bohanan, and they had a few pleasant words. He then found a bench and a watched the loading and unloading.

This gentleman lent a bit of class to the day. The roustabouts completed their task. Whenever there were people watching they would go into a little dance as they pushed their two wheel trucks.

Dinner 'lunch' was served about this time and we enjoyed the spot, soft crabs, spring chicken and vegetables which the cook had purchased that morning.

Dropping down to the river, we saw the Islands, St. Margaret's, St. Catherine's and the famed St. Clement's Island where the pilgrims to Maryland first landed.

The *Dorchester* fireman threw on extra coal and the black smoke came pouring from her stack and the paddle wheels seemed to churn harder and harder as we headed down the old Potomac River.

We rounded Piney Point and there were at the end of the long wharf, tied up at Tolson's Hotel. Several families disembarked for a few days stay. There was a nice sand beach there and bathers and sun lovers were enjoying it.

We admired the wool bathing suits and the ladies showing their figures to perfection, however, most of the children's cotton suits guaranteed to be dry like hung rags.

Passing St. George's Island we turned into the beautiful St. Mary's River and made the run up to the old Capitol of the State, St. Mary's City.

We tied up under the hill. This was indeed a deserted village. Here was no town, only a girl's school, the St. Mary's Female Seminary. As we dropped won the St. Mary's River, we looked back and could see the tall obelisk monument dedicated to the first Governor Maryland, Leonard Calvert. It was he who brought the first settlers to this land.

Hotel on the south side of
the First National bank in
Leonardtown 1929

Travelers leaving the steamboat at Leonardtown Wharf would make their way to the Hotel St. Mary's shown here in the center of town. Photo courtesy of Malcolm Morris.

Suddenly, the Captain turned to starboard. There was a wharf at the old plantation of Portobello. Someone had hoisted a broom up a pole on the end of the wharf which indicated there was freight to be picked up. At the wharf, we found one crate of old hens and a group of children.

The children rushed aboard and made straight for the ice cream chest. Shortly they happily went ashore licking their nickel cones. The steamboat was their only source of manufactured ice cream. We wondered how much begging they had engaged in to get their treat, their mother culling her old hens so they could entice the steamer to stop there.

Our next stop was at Grayson's Wharf on St. Inigoes Creek. Here the water was very deep right up to the bank and the wharf was almost on shore. The big trees in the yard of the very old "Cornwally Cross" Manor shaded the wharf.

Leaving Grayson's we circled the Jesuit Priest's farm on St. Inigoes Manor and soon were at the mouth of Smith's Creek. Here livestock was loaded, sheep and cattle. One rambunctious steer was giving the roustabouts trouble. Two had a rope attached to his horns and were on each side of the animal. Another was at the rudder (tail). They were putting on a big show for the passengers. The back man would twist the tail and the steer would leap and bellow.

Finally, he was loaded and the passengers gave applause for the show.

The Dorchester now crossed the wide Potomac to Virginia and proceeded up the Coan River so far that it finally ran out of water. There was a wharf at the bottom of a hill. I wondered how we would get out of this narrow headwater.

I soon found out.

A man and a small boat were put over he played out a little line as he rowed to the other side of the water. He pulls in the line that was attached to a hauser. He made several loops around a tall loblolly pine. The other end was attached the steamboats stern post. The vessel back and soon she had maneuvered a turn. The hauser was hauled in and the steamer churned down toward the mouth of the river.

Bottom sediment was stirred up and we left a dark wake.

The Northland steamer boasted this grand staircase.

There was a large wharf at the mouth of the river and a cannery was busy her at Lewisetta. They were working around the clock because this was the peak of the tomato season. We loaded hundreds of cases of canned tomatoes to be taken to Baltimore.

Finally as the sun sank behind the hills of Virginia's Northern Neck, we pulled into the Potomac.

At dusk, we rounded Point Lookout and headed north up the Chesapeake Bay.

Next morning we woke up at the Inner Harbor of Baltimore.

It had been a good trip.

Steamboats crowd the inner harbor of Baltimore, Md.

Sailing into Baltimore harbor in 2014. THE CHESAPEAKE TODAY photo

Chapter 25

BRINGING BACK THE LITTLE NIPPERS

By Cap'n Larry Jarboe
The Chesapeake

In the heart of downtown Piney Point on Rt. 249 is the machine shop owned by Joe Gardner. Should you need something fabricated, welded, brazed, ground, etched, threaded, bent, sheared, or cut, Joe can get the job done.

This October afternoon, he was cutting up some slab wood left over from a loblolly pine log that came from a right-of-way clearing job. He and his father cut the log into thick planks with Joe's chainsaw sawmill. The planks will be ripped into short handles for a very specialized oyster tong.

Joe is building iron nipper claws that bolt to the end of these handles. The nipper tong is a very small double claw tool that was used for picking up a single oyster at a time.

Today, the water is generally too murky for nipper tongs to work very well and oysters are not abundant enough for them to be effective. The nipper tongs that Joe is building will most likely go on display on someone's wall.

My only experience oyster tonging was with Wayne Suite on his big wooden charter boat formerly known as the Fishing Fun that he bought from Capt. Pete Ide. We borrowed a couple big tongs and headed out to the oyster bars off Benedict the first day of oyster season. With six people on board, we could recreationally harvest six bushels of oysters for the day. After working those tongs for a couple hours, we only had a half bushel to show for our efforts. That was the first and last time I ever tonged for oysters. Oyster diving is a far more effective way to gather oysters, but there is a catch.

Unfortunately, diving for oysters requires submerging your body into cold water. Those months with an "R" in them happen to be on the cool side of the calendar. Obviously, a wet suit is necessary. A dry suit is better. True professional oyster divers rig up a hose that pumps heated water into their wetsuits from the idling boat engine. With toasty warm water flowing through their suit, a working oyster diver can stay down for hours.

My dives on Patuxent River oyster bars have been educational but disappointing. Imagine a bottom covered with silted empty shells and minimum visibility. Every once in a while a living oyster will be found but that is only one edible mollusk for hundreds of dead shells. That is the way things were in the Patuxent off Solomon's Island twenty years ago. Today, the conditions are likely worse.

I enjoyed better diving for oysters in the Chesapeake Bay not far from the Calvert Cliffs Nuclear Power Plant. The water was generally much cleaner. Back then, there were clay lumps that were like big soft coral heads. Under the lumps and in holes within them, oysters grew fat in healthy groups. A clay lump could easily result in a full dive bag of

oysters.

Also, I ran a single oyster dive charter out of Chesapeake Beach for Capt. Ken Pumphrey aboard his wooden lapstrake charter boat named

This sketch from the Library of Congress shows the scene of the famous "Oyster Wars" which raged on the Potomac between Maryland and Virginia watermen right up until the 20th century. This scene depicts the time of about 1880. Oysters were so plentiful that they made those who controlled the business wealthy.

Patches. There are good reasons why I only ran a single trip for Capt. Ken but I will save that story for another issue of *The CHESAPEAKE.*

Perhaps, the most unique oyster boat I ever saw was hitched up to a horse heading west on Rt. 236. John Fisher had built a pontoon boat out of blue plastic barrels mounted under a wooden deck. He and a hearty group of fellow Amish men armed with oyster tongs launched the rig at the Wicomico Shores Public Landing. The wind was ripping pretty strong that day and the floating platform took off down the Wicomico River out of control.

They finally made shore at Chaptico Wharf. Of course, the horse was back at Wicomico Shores. A motor would have been nice but out of the question from the Elders' point of view.

Sadly, the glory days of bountiful oyster reefs are, at present, a thing of the past. We can hope that the new oyster sanctuary regulations introduced by Governor O'Malley and the Maryland Department of Natural Resources will be part of a greater solution that helps our Bay and rivers return to the bountiful estuaries they once were.

We have witnessed the return of the rockfish, might the oysters be next?

Huge mounds of oyster shells are next to this oyster packing house on the Wicomico River, in a photo from the 1930's when oysters were still plentiful. Photo from Library of Congress.

Chapter 26 Can't Miss: Sixteen Million Bricks Towering Above the Sea

By Cap'n Larry Jarboe
THE CHESAPEAKE

In April of 1980, my wife, Carlene, was a month pregnant with our first child. We decided to take a captain and mate's holiday from the boats we worked on at the Coral Reef State Park concession for a weekend in the Dry Tortugas. Dan and Cheryl LaCross, our best friends, agreed to join us on a 50 person charter that was organized by the Key Largo Historical Society.

Fort Jefferson is the naval fortress at the end of the Dry Tortugas island chain that has great historical significance to history buffs, especially Southern Marylanders. This is where Dr. Samuel Mudd from Charles County was interred for five years following the assassination of President Abraham Lincoln. The two-day weekend charter included round trip to and from Fort Jefferson with a cookout and camping on the boat or island. The seventy-mile voyage was only fifty bucks each. We were about the youngest couples booked on a boat full of senior citizens. I only remember one other young married couple with their elementary school age son.

The two and a half hour hundred mile trip from Key Largo to the Key West docks on the evening of Friday, April 11, 1980, was uneventful. We were anticipating a grand adventure but were a little concerned with the steady 25-knot wind that had been blowing from the East South East.

Our arrival at the party boat, *Can't Miss*, operated by Capt. Johnny Blackwell III was after dark, but it was easy to see this was a very old wooden boat. Dan was immediately ready to get his money back and return to Key Largo in his Dodge van with Cheryl, but I convinced him that, despite the worn appearance, this was a U.S. Coast Guard inspected vessel subject to rigorous oversight with a licensed captain who must know the limitations of his vessel.

I was wrong.

The night trip to the Tortugas was actually very smooth. Though the waves were running a height of 6-8 feet, the following sea nudged the stern of the 70' displacement hull boat in a gentle fluid motion. Somewhere through the course of the evening all of us got a little sleep on our bedrolls. We would need it later that weekend.

The sun was rising as we docked at the public pier at the Fort Jefferson National monument. This is a remarkable brick fortress which is a Nineteenth Century engineering marvel. The six-sided fort nearly completely covers Garden Key. Sixteen million bricks were used to build this massive structure that incongruously rises from the ocean in the middle of nowhere.

Immediately, we set about exploring inside the six walls of the fort. One of my favorite pictures from that day is me standing behind the bars on the door of Dr. Mudd's cell. Hopefully, that is the only time I will spend behind bars in this lifetime.

By lunchtime, as Carlene and Cheryl snacked on food from our cooler, Dan and I grabbed our spinning rods from the foc'sle and found a nice shady ledge under the docks to tempt mangrove snappers with some fresh shrimp. Normally, Mangrove Snappers are extremely wary. Though these fish might have gone to school, they had not been educated. We literally loaded the cooler with one pound to a pound and a half snappers. Boy were we going to have a great cookout that evening with fresh snapper for the grill!

With a cooler full of fish iced down, our crew of four castaways spent the afternoon snorkeling the soft coral reef that is on the lee side of the fort. There were plenty of tropical fish to entertain us along with bigger snappers and an occasional grouper. If not for our jobs in the real world, we were ready to just move on to the island.

There was one nagging observation that I had been watching all day. The U.S. flag above the fort was fully extended flying straight into the wind that was now closer to thirty knots.

When we returned to the boat late that afternoon to prep for the cookout, Capt. Blackwell notified us that the majority of the passengers wanted to go home. Dan said we had paid for a two-day trip and were looking forward to the evening on the island. The captain acknowledged but said the majority controlled the charter. I told him that he was going to be beating into small craft warning winds and rising seas. Why not make the crossing in the light of day as scheduled? Capt. Blackwell was determined to depart.

Around 6:30 P.M. that Saturday evening, we left the security of the Fort Jefferson docks for an open water crossing back to Key West. A beautiful day was going to turn into a very memorable night. The brilliant setting sun behind Fort Jefferson was little consolation to the coming tumble that I knew these groups of Historical Society patrons were going to endure to get back to the Key West docks.

By 8:00 P.M., the *Can't Miss* was pounding into 7-11 foot seas in the dark of night. We had positioned Cheryl in a center cabin location to try to rest as she was double dosed on Dramamine for her chronic seasickness. Many of the passengers were also feeling the effects of the roiling sea. The heads were full of barf and the acrid smell wafted through the cabin as Carlene and I played cards to pass the time. It was going to be a long night.

Carlene decided to go forward and grab a bunk in the foc'sle to take a snooze. When she looked below, bilge water had risen above the bottom bunks. The steps had broken off and were floating among loose debris in that compartment. A young man in the upper bunk got her attention and she helped him out of his stranded position. I believe he was the elementary school student who I spoke of in the first part of this narrative.

She notified Capt. Blackwell that there was a lot of water below and came back to tell me there about the high water in the bilge.

Capt. Blackwell slowed his boat down from the steady pounding he had maintained. The mate took over the helm and the captain went below deck to the engine room. He then went back to the helm, shut down one engine, grabbed a V-belt, and went back below. I told Carlene, "That darned fool broke an alternator belt and does not have a crossover to send juice from his other engine to charge batteries. This is one heck of a rotten time to be changing an alternator belt."

Capt. Blackwell showed my assessment was wrong.

He came from the depths of the engine room to announce to his weary passengers in the center cabin, "Folks, we have to start bailing!"

"His engine driven bilge pump is seized up," I told Carlene. "Find a bucket!"

There was no way to bail out the foc'sle as the water level was beyond an arm's reach. The water was knee deep in the next compartment between the foc'sle and the engine room. Armed with an aluminum cooking pot, I joined at least dozen other passengers and formed a bucket brigade to throw bilge water overboard from this central compartment. These men were mostly senior citizens from the Upper Keys who were now energized and organized to save the ship.

As we were bailing, passing full buckets and pots above, and returning the empty containers below, water washed from the deck above us onto our heads and shoulders.

"Guys, throw the water overboard," I called from the depths of the bilge.

"It's coming in from overboard!" was the reply from above us.

We quickly scampered up the steps to the stern which was sitting higher in the water.

Lifejackets were found by the passengers as the crew stayed holed up in the bridge. Word was passed back to the customers crowded on the stern that the Coast Guard had been called and a helicopter should arrive any minute with a pump.

Dan swept the decks on both sides of the boat clear by jettisoning coolers, seats, gear, or anything that might impede access from bow to stern. All those nice Mangrove Snappers we had caught earlier became fish food. We could be next.

I climbed atop the cabin to assess the condition of the floating life boat cushions. They were tied down tight in their racks. If the boat went down, they would go down with the boat.

I worked the knots loose on all the safety apparatus. As I made sure each cushion was free in its rack, I flipped up the flashing strobe light setting the light in motion. Ten or fifteen minutes later, about eight strobe lights were flashing from above the cabin.

The Coast Guard helicopter arrived soon after the strobes were set in motion but much later than we had expected. The LORAN coordinates called in by the crew were wrong. The helicopter was ten miles off course searching empty water when they spotted a Christmas display of flashing lights in the distance.

Dan and a senior passenger, I think his name was Fred, caught the Coast Guard enlisted man and pump dangling from a line below the chopper just before he nearly flew over the stern. The poor Coast Guard man was pretty shook up and disoriented, but he had done his job. The seniors grabbed the pump canister and took it to the forepeak at the bow. Like a well-oiled machine, the old timers pulled out the pump, assembled it, passed the suction hose into the bilge, and fired the sucker up. As water flowed from the depths of the Can't Miss overboard, we all cheered.

Dan helped the Coastie to a dry place in the cabin and pulled a tarp over him. The young rescuer was literally sick and tired and done for the night. Another pump was dropped by line in. The same precision team took over. Soon both pumps were humming. The water level started dropping and the bow came up from the sea.

Capt. Blackwell pushed ahead dead into the seven to eleven-foot seas toward Key West. With a light shining in the forepeak, we could see that the seams in his bow had opened up from the pounding seas. Each wave pushed in five gallons of water. We were only ten miles out of the safety of Fort Jefferson. I wondered why he did not do an 180 and take the safest course to land.

We manned the pumps all night. At daybreak, Dan and I looked over the starboard side to see a U.S. Coast Guard Cutter escorting us. We were still in open water, hardly halfway home. The men on board were laughing and joking. My buddy, Dan, could not take it anymore.

"Put a man on this boat now or we're going to mutiny and take this scum bucket back to Fort Jefferson." yelled Dan.

From the loudspeaker, the Coast Guard captain called back, "Those are not proper words from a crew."

"I'm a passenger; this captain has tried to kill me and everyone aboard this rotten heap. Now, send one of your boys over, NOW!" Dan screamed at the top of his lungs.

The cutter captain complied and moved alongside. One of his crew jumped aboard in a challenging maneuver.

Dan and I gave the Coast Guard crew member a tour of the vessel. We roused his fellow crewman from under the tarp. We then turned the vessel over to their care and joined our wives in the cabin.

About two or three o'clock on Sunday afternoon, a very weary group of refugees arrived at the Key West docks on the Can't Miss.

Capt. Blackwell and his crew who had done nothing to assist their passengers or keep the boat afloat were now quickly trying to send the customers home. All our gear was scattered deep in the foc'sle among the broken bunks and steps. We were not going anywhere without our belongings.

Dan and I eased our bodies over the doorway and dropped into the bilge. We pulled out our dive gear, oily fishing rods, and extra clothes. The sleeping bags were shredded and completely worthless. We passed our stuff up and pulled ourselves back up to the main deck.

As we sorted our soiled belongings on the dock, a local charter captain walked by and complained that we were messing up the docks with our junk. After nearly forty hours with no sleep, I had to hold Dan back from clobbering the guy. We did not need to spend time in a Key West jail for assault.

The Coast Guard pulled Capt. Blackwell's Certificate of Inspection that day. He was only rated for twenty miles offshore. The seventy-mile passage he booked was in extreme violation of the boat's credentials.

Dan and I testified at the Coast Guard hearing along with other passengers. Capt. Johnny Blackwell III lost his tonnage license. He appealed the decision, but he did not get his license back.

However, word drifted up the Keys that Johnny Blackwell III took his non-certificated heap of a boat out of dry dock only a few days after trying to drown fifty people on a Historical Society expedition.

The story is that he made three runs to Cuba in the Mariel Boatlift. Each trip imported 150 Cubans at a thousand bucks a head. The cash money was used to buy a fiberglass version of the Can't Miss that still operates out of the Key West docks.

Piracy is alive and well today for anyone venturing to Key West, Florida.

Florida grunts caught by the barrel. Photo by Cap'n Larry Jarboe

The Country Philosopher
By
Stephen Gore Uhler

THE AUTHORITY ON GOOD SENSE

CHAPTER 27
PONZI POLITICIANS, TV MINISTERS, SOCIALISTS AND TREE-HUGGERS

When Jack Rue so selfishly dropped dead and stuck me with this column, I knew it would not be easy.

Oh sure, I possess the superior intellect, years of on-hand experience, I have such unflagging physical stamina, and in all modesty, I admit to the manly good looks and charming ways with which I have been blessed.

In short, I did not approach this job with trepidation because of any lack of confidence in my own ability, but I did remember the old adage that a prophet "is without honor in his own country."

Being a Philosopher, Prophet, Guru, or wise man of any description has never been easy.

Remember the Biblical prophets; God tested them with all kinds of boils. He left them sitting on dunghills with sore loins and barren wives. No, the Lord God did not cut his prophets any slack. Even those prophets whom God seemed to favor were always wandering around in the desert pulling down golden calves and breaking up false idols.

And don't forget that sprinkled among the true prophets; there have always been those false prophets, nefarious fellows who use their talents to prey upon their brethren of lower intellect.

I won't try to go back into antiquity to cite all the "wise guys" who fed false data to the Pharaoh's and were always selling their brothers into slavery and getting their beautiful sisters to seduce wealthy Kings. The ancient writings are full of conspiracies and intrigue. We could never tell it all in this brief column.

Moving ahead into the twentieth century, we find this guy, Mr. Ponzi. Mr. Ponzi was a bright, enterprising fellow who ran ads in all the papers to announce that if willing investors would merely send him a certain small sum of money, he would return them unimaginable riches. The plan worked wonderfully. As more and more investors responded to the ads, Mr. Ponzi was able to pay off the early investors at a phenomenal rate of return. Unfortunately, as with anything that grows exponentially, the scheme soon used up the supply of new investors, at which time Mr. Ponzi scooped up the money on hand and fled back to Italy and retired in wealth and splendor.

Ever since then such bamboozles have been called "Ponzi Schemes".

Another false Prophet came along a few years later and thought he could improve on the Ponzi scheme.

F.D.R. came up with "social security" which a republican senator declared was neither "social nor secure."

F.D.R. proposed to take a few pennies each week out of the paycheck of those working and give it to those not working. It worked fine as long as about 50 workers were contributing to the income of 1 retiree.

Now the Ponzi Scheme or social security has come full circle and you have one worker keeping 2 or 3 retirees, and not just in bread and sustenance, but in Medicaid, Medicare, meals on wheels, heart bypasses, prostate reaming's, and Viagra. I can't wait until my 2 little grandsons get out there and start keeping me in the style to which I would like to become accustomed.

This entire prelude has been to remind the reader that there have always been true Prophets and false Prophets and even the wisest of us have difficulty distinguishing the rightful path to follow.

I still kick myself when I realize the thousands of dollars I sent to the Rev. Jimmy Swaggart over the years to feed the hungry little children he so tearfully displayed on T.V., only to find that he spent the money in whorehouses.

I could have spent the money in the whorehouse myself and cut out the middleman.

But, enough about Prophets, ancient and modern, and their feet of iron and clay. Let's talk about here and now.

I told you people when Joe Anderson filed for county commissioner that you were dealing with a left-wing, tree hugging, washed out Vista volunteer who could only bring this fair county to grief.

I use the term, "tree hugger" as a pejorative to distinguish the ersatz environmentalist from the true lover of nature.

The "tree hugger" only enforces the bureaucratic environmental rules on others while the true environmentalist is as strict with himself as he would be on others, probably more so.

For three centuries, our hardy ancestors have protected this frail peninsula.

We took of the bounty of our fields and estuaries as we needed and left the rest to increase.

The rivers were full of crabs, fish, and oysters, the fields were full of rabbits, quail and deer. The fields and woods were also full of "skeeters", chiggers, ticks, fleas and "no-seem-ums."

Nature was in balance, the small birds and fishes fed on the tiny pest and were in turn eaten by the larger fish and animals, and thus nature remained bountiful.

Now these ersatz environmentalists would spray our fields and forests with deadly chemicals and upset that delicate balance.

Back in the "good old days" when I ran barefoot across field and stream, every brook and puddle was inhabited by frogs. I did not say some brooks and puddles, I said every.

As we crept through the forest, we knew that at every puddle we approached we would hear the "kerplunk" as frogs dived for cover.

We didn't have to carry a watch to know when evening was nigh, because as every schoolboy knew when evening was nigh the whip-poor-will would call. I haven't heard a whip-poor-will all summer.

Why?

Because phony tree huggers have killed all the "skeeters" upon which the whip-poor-wills feed.

Why does Joe Anderson want to spray our mosquitoes?

So that he can turn his delicate, pink ass up on the beach unmolested.

Back in the "good old days" when nature was in balance, a person going out knew he would have to swat "hoss flies" in the morning, sheep flies in mid-day and "skeeters" in the evening. They came with the game.

One delicate little creature I have not seen for years is the "spring keeper". In the "good old days" before Metcom and the Health Department, we would carry up our water from springs dug on hillsides in the forest. A fresh flowering vent would be dug out and lined with bricks to make a pool where the sweet water could be dipped. Every such spring was inhabited by one little grey and white salamander. They must have been very territorial because there would always be only one to a spring, and every spring had its spring keeper.

The spring keeper would dart about the spring eating little bits of algae and insects which might fall into the spring, keeping the water crystal clear.

You had to be careful when dipping your pail not to catch the spring, keeper.

A spring without a spring keeper would soon turn cloudy with detritus.

When we kids would set the pails of fresh water on the stand, Mama would check in the buckets to be sure we hadn't accidentally caught the spring, keeper. A spring keeper swimming in the water bucket meant a long walk back down the hill to return him.

We kids would ask boyish questions like, "if the spring keeper is born in the spring and lives all his life in the spring, where does he go to the bathroom?"

Shush! That's not for children to know.

But now, alas, there are no more frogs and salamanders, whip-poor-wills, skeeters, gnats, chiggers, fleas, leeches, bedbugs.

We live in this sterile environment with no need to swat or scratch. "Gypsy Joe" and his band of phony environmentalists can crowd our beaches with their delicate, pink asses turned up to the sun.

Delicate pink, without pimple or pustule, no buzzing, no croaking, no noisy whip-poor-wills.

The main business route of Salisbury, Maryland has a draw span. THE CHESAPEAKE Photo

The flags ever wave from the Town Pier at Crisfield, Md. THE CHESAPEAKE TODAY photo

CHAPTER 28 **FROM MONSTER FISHING TO A MESS OF FISH**

One of the great advantages of living in the Chesapeake Bay region is having the opportunity for almost anyone to catch a trophy striped bass during the Spring and Fall migrations. A few years ago, prior to the five-year moratorium on striped bass harvest established during Governor Donald Schaefer's tenure, you were lucky if you even caught a small striped bass. Now, we all have a shot at catching a big rockfish.

In June, most of those big fish will have moved on. If you want to catch a monster, the cow nose skates are prowling everywhere or you might target the big blue catfish that have moved into the fresher portion of the Potomac River. I expect there may be a patient fisherman or two prepping to go shark fishing after witnessing the bull sharks caught in the pound nets last year.

For most of us, June through October is a numbers game. The fish may not be so big, but you can catch a cooler full which is a whole lot of family fun. I admit this is my favorite kind of fishing. Pulling in a big striped bass on a trolling rig is like trying to reel in an open five-gallon bucket being dragged behind the boat. Give me a double header of croakers coming up on a light spinning rig any day. Compound that experience surrounded by your friends all catching fish on their bottom or chumming rigs and you have the makings of a grand day of fishing.

In years past, I was a purist, well actually just cheap, and tied my own double hook bottom rigs using dropper knots. These rigs often tangle which wastes valuable fishing time. The wire spreader bottom rigs that you buy tangle far less and the clip for the sinker makes lead changing quick and easy. Remember, that having three hooks on a single line is illegal for recreational fishing in Maryland. Also, another trick I learned quite by accident is to fish a wire spreader double hook bottom rig without a lead drifted behind an anchored boat.

Last August, I needed some fish pictures for the CHESAPEAKE and took an early morning trip out on the Patuxent River. The white perch were biting pretty well, but they were running in the small category. My sinker hung on the bottom and the clip and sinker broke off leaving me with a two hook wire spreader rig and no weight.

So, I cast the baited but non-weighted rig behind the boat, flipped out a lot of slack line, and put the rod in the stern rod holder with an open bail while I baited up a bottom rig on another rod. By the time I got that rig to the bottom, the drift rig rod was jumping. I pulled in two big croakers on that rig and proceeded to catch my limit of croaker on the drift rig. I think the wire spreader has enough weight to drift to the bottom and move across with the current. Regardless of why it works, this is a good trick that you are welcome to forget, but a smart fisherman won't.

Regardless of whether you are catching one or two fish at a time, June is the time to catch a nice mess of fish with minimum effort. If you can't catch them now, you might as well take up playing golf.

Snakehead fish brought into Buzz's Marina in Ridge.

Bull Shark caught near swimming beach at Point Lookout State Park was brought into Buzz's Marina for weighing and touching.
Photo for THE CHESAPEAKE courtesy of Buzz's Marina.

A great skate was part of the day's catch for a skatefish tournament on the Patuxent River. ***THE CHESAPEAKE photo by Cap'n Larry Jarboe***

CHAPTER 29
"SWEET THING" & A .44 MAGNUM

Being a child of the Great Depression, brought up during the time of WWII, I was born and raised in a tough time.

Now, sixty years later, the cold war with the threat of immediate nuclear incineration having worn us out, I suppose I have a good share of insecurity.

We insecure people develop mechanisms for coping. Like Linus with his blanket, we cling to our security fetishes. I always found my security in the wad of cash in my pocket.

In the early days, I couldn't have a wad of real cash. I would have to cut newspapers into the right size wrap and wrap a couple of twenties around the outside. To the general observer, I gave the appearance of being a well-financed young man.

When dickering for horse feed, new boots, machinery or any of the necessities that I must have or must acquire, I would pull my wad out from time to time and riffle it just enough to show the corners of the two twenties on the outside, being careful not to expose the newsprint that formed the base of my financial empire.

"That boy came ready to do business."

As I gradually built my investments by advantageous use of my show money and a lot of fast talk, my friends would hint that perhaps I should think of using checks or even credit cards, but as I explained earlier, I am a child of the Great Depression determined that no bank would ever close with my money inside. Credit cards I didn't even consider, as Granddaddy would say, "Pay as you go, if you can't pay don't go!"

Somebody's going to knock you in the head "someday" my friends would warn. That was the least of my worries. In addition to the words of wisdom, my granddaddy had also bequeathed me his 1915 model Iver-Johnson .32 special. It was not much of a pistol, probably cost $5 back then.

It would be a "Saturday Night Special" these days, but it did have hand carved ivory handgrips instead of the cheap, slippery molded plastic grips on today's weapons.

I had accumulated an excess of ammo over the years and one day I decided to go to the range and shoot away all of the green, corroded cartridges and just keep about 100 of the most recently purchased bullets.

So, there I was at the range, just firing away.

I was shooting at a man - sized target and just nicking the edges every once in a while. I wasn't really trying with my bent up, rusty old relic, just busting caps and having fun when this high stepping red-head took the target next to mine and put six or seven bullets through the right eye of her automatic rapid fire, shoved in a fresh clip, switched hands and shot out the other eye.

She rolled her big blue eyes at me and then at my barely nicked target. "Stay Cool," I thought, that's too fine a trophy to spook."

"I'm just shooting some old ammo through this antique to get rid of it. Let me fire that thing you got, and I'll show you what a good marksman can do."

"I can't let you," she replied.

She must have seen my gills turning red because she hastily added, "This is one of those new smart weapons that can only be fired by me."

I took her pistol in my best military stance, aimed, and nothing happened.

"See, you didn't believe me. This weapon has a computer in the grip, which instantly reads the D.N.A. of the person holding it. If that person is not me, the gun won't fire.

I didn't want to shoot her fancy pistol with the cheap plastic grips, anyway. I just wanted to get next to her and break the ice. I must have done a pretty good job of icebreaking, within a week, she and the fancy pistol and the big blue eyes, were regular fixtures in my bachelor's pad.

"Sweetie," she asked me as I was rolling out one morning to go to work, "Sweetie would you drop my pistol off at the gunsmith."

"You got that thing broke up already?"

"No, silly boy, I'm having it fitted with laser sights. I'll just have to put that red dot on my target, and night or day, bingo."

WHICH WAY TO ST. GEORGE'S ISLAND?

Well, her mind is a little too "high tech" for me, but the rest of her is as primitive as Eve in the Garden. I'd better get her gun to the shop.

But that left me with a problem. I couldn't just drop her gun in my pocket with my trusty .32 Iver-Johnson and I didn't want to jam it in the other side on top of my money roll.

So, I tossed my faithful old weapon in a drawer and left for work with just her new-fangled gadget.

Wouldn't you know it! I have traveled on three oceans and four continents, into the most dark and dreary alleys you could imagine and there it was.

A stickup man waving a gun in my face in downtown L.P. City.

I was startled at first, especially since the young stick-up man was so obviously a novice.

"Give it up! Give it up!", as he waved a big .44 magnum right in my face.

He must have stolen that gun from Clint Eastwood. The best-looking pistol I've ever seen and then I noticed he still had the trigger lock in.

The dumbbell, I thought, he doesn't even know his gun is locked. I ought to waste the dummy right here in broad daylight. I eased my hand into my pocket as if to give him my money, but really I intended to fill him with slugs from my little Iver-Johnson.

Damn! I thought as I felt the slimy molded plastic of "Sweet Things" smart gun. I am as helpless as he is. I figured I'd psyche him out.

"Your trigger's locked, you dumb bastard." It was his turn to be flustered.

He ran his left hand into his left pocket and groped. He switched hands and groped with his right hand, and then he laid the big hog leg on the sidewalk and groped with both hands. No key!

He was so intent on finding his key; the poor fool didn't realize that he could bash my brains out with that monstrosity and just stroll away with my money.

I had had enough and was feeling the urge to giggle. I didn't think it would be wise to giggle in the face of a desperate robber. So, I leveled "Sweet Things" high tech 9 mm right between his eyes.

"Sucka, you gonna die."

He set the record for the 100-yd. dash and left me the proud owner of a brand new .44 Magnum.

It took me about 2 minutes in my shop to drill out the trigger lock. The drill bit cut through the lock like cheese cake.

Every time "Sweet Thing" and I go to the pistol range, now I have to thank Gov. Glendening, Billy Boy Clinton, "Spendy Hoyer" and the rest of the left-wing, lying lefties for this nice magnum. I would never be so extravagant to buy it for myself, but since God in his wisdom placed it right at my feet, I intend to use it.

I let "Sweet Thing" go first.

Pow! Pow! Pow!

And then I take my turn.

Kaboom! Kaboom! Kaboom!

The first edition of THE CHESAPEAKE published in August of 1988 was dedicated to Buck Briscoe.

Seven Gables Hotel on the Patuxent. Below, shortly before being razed for construction of a boatel; it was once one of more than a dozen hotels lining the shores of St. Mary's County, Md.

Photos for The Chesapeake by Darrin Farrell.

CHAPTER 30 **REVENGE OF THE BASSER**

National Roving Fish Reporter
By Frank the Beachcomber

The Bass-O-Reno was just about the best fishing lure you could own when I was a young man. I should know. I was about eighteen and knew all the answers, and had the credentials to prove it. I lived in a part of Chicago, where the kids represented more nationalities than there are in Europe, and every one of them was scrambling to earn spending money. By doing any kind of a job they could find, and being of the same breed I was conning a select group into paying some of it back to me for the honor of belonging to the Timber Wolves Outdoor Club. The Bass-O-Reno just happened to win our attention because it was so good at catching bass in the Pine Creek Flowage --- way up north in Wisconsin. To us, going up there for a few summers was like going to MECCA. As it turned out one summer, it was not without its perils.

But getting up to Pine Creek was a story in itself, because it was three hundred miles from Chicago, and there was no such thing as using the family car. If you wanted to go on a vacation, you just had better try to figure out a way to do it. Being one of six boys I had figured it out, and so the Timber Wolves were formed. It was only a matter of months and scheming before we had a small wall tent, a basic conglomeration of camp gear and a master plan.

Being the owner of the Model "A", I naturally was the president, laid down all the rules. Everyone pitched in for gas, food and boat rentals. Three members fished from a boat at a time and alternated rowing. Only two fellows fished at a time, which of course at times could be a real test of endurance for the fellow at the oars. I know because I was stuck on the job one day, deep in the sticks of the Pine Flowage. Kids have a habit of getting as deep as possible into a jungle like this because it always seems to be so much better farther away. This was during the days before we owned an outboard motor, and rowing through a flowage can be a tedious job. Luckily we were a versatile group, and we usually carried a lot of little tools, for jury-rigging jobs that are a part of surviving while camping. Fortunately for us it saved the day.

Elmer was a Swedish kid who had a part-time job helping electricians and enjoyed flaunting a pair of heavy-duty wire cutters he used in his work. As might be expected, on this day he had left them in camp. It was during the excitement of a bass strike that the unexpected happened.

Now I was just an ordinary kid at heart, in reality. The temptation just became more than I could stand. I grabbed my casting rod, waved the Bass-O-Reno over my head and let it fly. There seemed to be an agonizing moment as I waited the "PLOP" when the lure was supposed to hit the water. But as my eyes went searching for an answer my heart almost stopped, for inches from my face I could see my Bass-O-Reno hanging from the ear of Elmer. One barb had gone through the lobe while a barb from another set of hooks was embedded in a fleshy part above. One glance told me there was no way anyone could twist those barbs loose.

Silence is golden they say, and there was plenty of it as we headed back through the stumps toward camp and the pair of wire cutters.

A lot of things have changed since that day, and a lot of water has flowed through the Pine Creek Flowage. The Timber Wolves have disbanded, and the last time I looked I had six growing sons. Only the Pine Creek Flowage seems the same, only now my sons have been honing their fishing skills. Joe, my eighteen-year-old, was the one who was rowing on that second fateful day. Of course, by now we had an outboard to get us deep into the sticks.

Strangely enough, even after all those years, the Bass-O-Reno was still my favorite lure, and while I worked the stumps vigorously, Joe had his lure on stand-by, inches from his hand. Of course, other changes had taken place in my own lifestyle. The bright red handkerchief I used to tie to my forehead had now been replaced by a slouchy straw hat to keep the sun off my shiny head, and a light sweater kept me warmer, where at one time I was always searching for a heavy tan. My commanding tones of authority had also been replaced by kindly suggestions, but that inner excitement that comes with a bass or northern hitting a lure never completely escapes one.

This day with Joe was really one to remember. The sun creeping over the placid green water painted the stumps and sticks into an ancient cemetery mural. The dead silence was interrupted only by the far off cry of a crow, or car spinning along on the county road that circled the flowage.

For me, every twist through the labyrinth of sprawling stumps and quiet bay was a trip back into time. There were moments when I could drift back into memories, of campfires and soggy tents, and starchy spaghetti along with congealed rice, and coffee that represented ink and tasted like it. Every twist and turn marked some spot that we either had caught a big bass or had one get away just as we were ready to land it.

There is something about being detailed to row that has a way of leaving your feelings mirrored on your face. I knew I was due to row, but I still was itching to see just one bass hit my lure, and so I kept shooting side-long glances at Joe while I wondered how far I could push his patience.

I didn't have long to wait. Bass have a habit of exploding when you least expect them to. It was a picture postcard spot.

A great ancient stump sprawling in all directions, surrounded by limpid green water with a few water lilies for decoration. I arched my red and white lure in a gentle sweep and watched the ripples undulate in an ever-widening circle and the lure went sailing into the air with a big bronze back attached to it ....

What happened then was an episode that took me back twenty-five years and I sat stunned trying to believe it was actually true. I knew I was aware of Joe grabbing his rod, leaning back and putting all his energy into the perfect cast, but the sudden nerve-wracking tug of my scalp under my straw hat told me the lure would never see water.

I am an explosive guy at times and used to have a choice collection of words for specific occasions, but now I seemed to be stripped of all but a few "Joe, I said, trying to be calm, while I wondered about my options, "will you see if you can out pull this thing out of my head.?"

For some strange reason, Joe seemed to have suddenly lost his beautiful summer tan, as he sat stunned next to me. Slowly he reached for my straw hat and gave the Bass-O-Reno a tug and for the first time in my life, I learned how thick the skin of your skull can be.

Thank God for outboard motors and cars that start when you need them. We even actually go to see a doctor without too much waiting, even though he didn't seem too impressed by a guy with a straw hat anchored to his head by a bright red and white plug.

Don't let it bother you," he said with a big grin. "You're not the only fellow that I've untangled this year. I know when the fishing season starts the parade starts. In fact, I have a trophy case at home with souvenir lures I've dug out of fishermen in the last ten years".

A boy and his dog ready for a day of fishing. Andrew Rossignol and Nike.
THE CHESAPEAKE photo

Point Lookout, Maryland. This photo shows the confluence of the Chesapeake Bay and the Potomac River. *THE CHESAPEAKE photo by Darrin Farrell*

Thickets, Forests and Meadows

Life, Liberty and the Pursuit of Wildlife

BY RICH JOHNSON
OUTDOOR LIFE WRITER

CHAPTER 31
HUNT DEER "DANIEL BOONE" STYLE

By Rich Johnson
The Chesapeake

As I sit in my living room typing this hunting article, I am enjoying the warmth from my woodstove and know full well it is currently in the teens outside. Last I looked it was 18 degrees. It is definitely cold enough to quickly freeze your extremities if you are not properly clothed. These low temperatures will not make deer hunting very comfortable if you are not well prepared.

Even though it is cold outside, deer still have to eat and will venture out to get some chow. I mention this for deer season is still open till the end of January for Crossbow. I had contemplated possibly going crossbow hunting this Saturday evening, but the cold was not too encouraging. Plus I had rather stay home for now and tend to my sick 5-year-old son, who looks to be making a quick recovery.

Now I do plan to do some late season crossbow hunting and I think you should too for I don't think many hunters will be out working the woods. Fewer hunters in the woods will make the deer less spooked and allow a better chance of bagging one last deer.

Since sitting in a tree stand in these cold temperatures is not very comfortable, when you sit still for a long time your body temperature will start to fall. So in addition to not being comfortable, you may get overexposure which is something you should like to avoid. So what do you do in these last days of crossbow and not freeze your butt in the process? I recommend hunting what I call "Daniel Boone" style. It can be productive and keep you warm.

What I call "Daniel Boone" style is basically a very slow stalk through the woods. It reminds me of the time I was a kid watching Fess Parker in the Daniel Boone series as he would sneak up on the game with a well-concealed stalk.

Of course Fess Parker always got his deer, but I had to develop a method that would allow me to get mine.

What I developed is a trek into the thick laurel and I aim for a large tree for cover as I slowly stalk through the woods.

Now if you have never stalked before and don't know how fast you move, here is an example. Say you have your arm next to your side and have an itchy nose and need to scratch it.

Well, once you start to move your arm to get that nose scratched, the total time should be no less than a minute.

Plus while you are doing this slow movement, your eyes are constantly scanning the area for movement and your ears are listening for anything.

If anything is detected, you must immediately cease movement and zero in on the game before they detect you. You also need to know where your feet will be placed that will make the minimum noise. One break of a twig will scare off your deer.

I usually stalk up to the tree I selected for cover, and wait a few minutes. If nothing is detected, I pick my next tree I will use for cover and re-start my slow stalk once again. This slow movement will stress your muscles and keep you warm. I have used this method and was able to get a shot at an 8 point buck.

So try some "Daniel Boone" style hunting. You have a good chance to bag that deer and will keep warm in the process. Get that deer and be safe.

The Captain Sam Bailey in the Potomac River.
THE CHESAPEAKE photo

CHAPTER 32 **YOUR GREAT ESCAPE**

By Cap'n Larry Jarboe
The Chesapeake

When you wake up in the morning to cold rain and snow in our Chesapeake Bay watershed, believe it or not, the weather is warm and the sun is shining in the Caribbean. Southern Marylanders live in a world class cruising, fishing, and water sports area for most of the year. However, the winter months can inflict a severe case of cabin fever for those of us addicted to having a deck beneath our feet.

In past years, I simply growled and scowled my way through the winter months as I woke before sunrise and worked outside past sunset in weather that was simply miserable. For over a quarter century; been there, done that, not going back. Now, I plan my annual escape and welcome you to do the same.

Cap'n Larry looks for the 5 cent machines in the casino, but all he found was the art gallery. ***THE CHESAPEAKE photo***

This year, my wife and I took a 12-day trip out of Baltimore with Celebrity Cruise Lines aboard the MV Mercury to the Eastern Caribbean.

We missed the cold weather through the middle of January and snorkel dove the waters of five islands. While people across our Country were shoveling snow, Carlene and I were flipping our swim fins over tropical reefs, sipping cold island beers, and soaking up the sun for a nice healthy tan.

A trip like this does not have to be expensive. Interior and even some ocean view cabins can be booked for less than fifty bucks a day per person if you watch for the cruise specials that are available.

All of the islands have taxi service that will take you to the beachfront swimming, snorkeling, and diving areas. By skipping the cruise ship excursions and planning your own custom trip, you can significantly reduce your costs.

Check out as much you can on the Internet before you get on board your cruise ship. Onboard Internet rates are simply unreasonable.

You can catch up with your e-mails at the Internet cafes when you reach your destination.

Unless you have pressing business, avoid making a shipboard connection. Use your home service to cruise the Net before boarding and enjoy your cruise without worrying about how much searching the Web is going to cost you.

Another expense that you can do without is the roaming charge on your cell phone. Turn it off.

But!!! Remember to wear a watch.

Many of us now depend on our cell phones for the time of day.

Better yet, wear a dive watch. You will not have to take it off in the water and it will help you not lose track of time should you become engrossed with natural beauty of the tropical marine ecosystem or the French ladies swimming off the topless beach.

Though you are on vacation, you must stay abreast of your schedule to arrive back to the ship prior to departure.

Our particular cruise of the Eastern Caribbean included five single-day stops at the islands of St. Thomas, St. Croix, St. Kitts, Antigua, and St. Maarten. The goal of this trip was to bring back detailed information about the most affordable and accessible beaches to visit and snorkel in the Caribbean. I made the mistake of not doing a good Internet search prior to getting on the cruise.

Fortunately, my years of experience running commercial passenger carrying vessels helped me ask the right questions on each island to find the best snorkeling beaches to share with readers of the CHESAPEAKE.

During our first stop in St. Thomas, Carlene and I struck off from our cruise party of St. Mary's County residents interested in shopping extravaganzas to find the best beach to see coral and marine life close to shore.

The general consensus from the local people and taxi drivers was Coki Beach, which is across the island from where the cruise ships dock. After a nice tour of the island by taxi, we arrived at Coki Beach. Immediately, we were hustled to rent beach chairs. We settled on one to keep our gear together.

If I had done an Internet search earlier, I would have known that a 14-year-old girl who was a passenger on the Carnival Cruise Line was shot and killed nearby in July of last year.

Though ignorance may be bliss, I picked up on a strange vibe at this beach with the vendors who continually pushed to give body massages or hair braiding. Carlene and I took turns guarding our gear while the other one of us went into the water.

The marine life near this beach which is adjacent to the Coral World Marine Park is quite good for a shore access. The coral outcropping right off the beach is full of tropical marine fish and some of the fattest yellowtail snappers I have ever seen so close to land.

A Google search of [Coki Beach fish feeding frenzy] will give you a good view of the beach as well as the variety of fish and corals that you will see a very short swim from shore.

The local people sell crackers to feed the fish which accounts for the friendliness of the fish as well as the fatness of the snappers. Those carbs really bulk up the yellowtails.

The islander vendors also recommended that tourists leave the beach after 3:00 P.M. for safety.

Actually, I think they had a big local celebration cooking for the evening and did not want a culture mix that could cause more bad press.

Dead tourists are not good for business.

Regardless, we knew it was time to get out of Dodge by dodging out of Coki Beach in a taxi.

All in all, Coki Beach was the best beach for a novice snorkeler, but I would recommend traveling in a group because it is not the safest of places on the shore side.

The next stop became my favorite dive site of the trip which is Cane Bay in St. Croix. This time we were joined by our full party of cruising friends.

After haggling with the taxi drivers over rates, we walked into the nearby Cane Bay Dive Shop right beside the cruise ship docks. For four dollars less than the round trip of a taxi, they provided the complete two-way taxi trip, snorkel gear, beach chairs and very detailed directions on the best snorkeling and diving areas.

Apparently, the dive shop offered the best deal which got even better as you will see.

The friendly folks at the Cane Bay Dive Shop on St. Croix had the best snorkeling and the best rum punch. THE CHESAPEAKE photo

After a scenic trip across the island, we were fortunate to arrive on an almost flat calm day with a hundred foot of visibility in the blue water. Cane Bay is at the edge of a deep 3,000-foot drop off which provides a shore diving experience unmatched by anything I have witnessed.

Though this trip was dedicated to snorkeling, I intend to come back to spend a few days in St. Croix specifically enjoying the scuba diving if they will accept my 40-year-old PADI dive certification card.

The vibe at this beach was laid back and the snorkeling was excellent for strong swimmers. I would recommend a safety vest because of the distance the best reef areas are from shore. Especially beautiful is the deep drop that extends down into the dark blue water. I was reminded of snorkeling in Okinawa in another place in time. But, that is another story.

One thing that many people notice in the Caribbean waters close to populated areas is the relative lack of food fish like grunts and porgies and larger fish like groupers or big snappers. There is a reason for this which I will reveal later. However, the underwater structure of Cane Bay makes this a destination worth spending more time at.

After exploring the reef, we went back to enjoy time on the beach. During a conversation with David and Katie from West Virginia who came in on another taxi, we discovered there was free rum punch nearby provided by the dive shop for our after dive enjoyment. A lively conversation ensued and the day went from really very good to even better.

David and Katie were a young married couple who were also cruising on the *Mercury*. The Cane Bay excursion was the beginning of more new snorkeling friendships we made on the trip. Our gratitude goes to

Suzanne Rosbach, owner of Cane Bay Dive Shop for her supreme hospitality and strong rum punch!

Upon arrival at St. Kitts, we hooked up with our past cruise tour guide and driver, Captain Kenny Sunshine, to take us across the island to Cockleshell Beach. This beach has thousands of shells in shallow snorkeling depth. You can spend hours searching for colorful Caribbean shells or you can swim to the rock outcroppings from the point to see shallow corals and fish. There is a lot of trash on the bottom which degrades the snorkeling experience, but my wife swam with a spotted eagle ray and a squid which was the highlight snorkeling experience of her trip. Again, the massage and hair braiding vendors were out in force along with hucksters of cheap jewelry.

Carlene gives thumbs up to the great massage at St. Kitts. THE CHESAPEAKE photo

St. Kitts does have the most breathtaking view of the volcanic mounts during the trip to and from the beach. You can see both the Atlantic and the Caribbean waters at the same time. Though they may look the same from a passing ship, each Caribbean island has its own unique culture and ambiance.

Long Bay was the highly recommended beach in Antigua, which was our next port. This time, Carlene and I were again on our own so the taxi ride was a little more expensive. Ideally, find a group to get the best rate. The trip across the island was enjoyable. The new Antigua sports stadium is covered with solar panels which are a very practical addition to this land where the sunshine is the predominate order of the day.

What time is the midnight buffet? Carlene and Larry Jarboe plan on making this lunch last.

The reef at Long Bay is close to shore, but the facilities to change clothing are limited to the bathrooms of the local bar. It is better to wear your bathing suit underneath your clothes on most of these excursions. The Long Bay reef area was fine for snorkeling, but the local vendor

pressure especially the illicit offer to purchase "smoke or coke" made the beach unappealing to me. Other than the presence of more cruise ship new acquaintances, Pam and Peter, Long Bay will become a long gone memory.

The most secure, clean, and scenic beach of our trip was on Pinel Island on the French side of St. Maarten. After a pleasant taxi trip across the island where we quickly passed through the Dutch/French border, our group of new snorkeling friends and accomplices boarded a small passenger ferry to cross a short distance to Pinel Island which is a park and marine sanctuary. On the island, there were shore lockers for safe storage of our gear which is a welcome benefit. Also, no vendors pushed to sell their goods. There was calm protected water to fish watch in. I walked to the open ocean side of the island and snorkeled in the surf to see the larger coral formations.

On the swim out to the reef, there was the frame of a defunct fish trap. The wire mesh had been removed. This is the reason why there are so few food and large fish on the Caribbean reefs. The island fishermen continue to use these traps to deplete what few fish they have left. A fish trap acts like a vacuum cleaner that literally sucks up fish much like the bank traps we banned in St. Mary's County over a decade ago. I expect these traps are illegal in the marine sanctuary of Pinel Island, but it will take quite a few years for the fish to repopulate the area.

Cane Bay on St. Croix gets high marks for both diving and snorkeling.
THE CHESAPEAKE photo

That said, the peaceful serenity of Pinel Island along with the natural beauty of topless sunbathers certainly will leave pleasant memories for many years to come. Sipping a cold Red Stripe beer under a thatch roof hut with new found friends was the perfect way to end our last shore excursion.

Maybe you might like to take a couple weeks off from the chill of winter to chill out with a Caribbean cruise. The prices are extremely affordable and the weather there is sunny and warm. Are you ready now to start planning your escape?

This is the proper way to spend January after working hard all year. The island of Nevis as seen from a beach chair on St. Kitts.

THE CHESAPEAKE photos by Ken Rossignol

A traditional fishing boat in the Caribbean. THE CHESAPEAKE photo

CHAPTER 33 A BUCKET FULL OF ADVICE

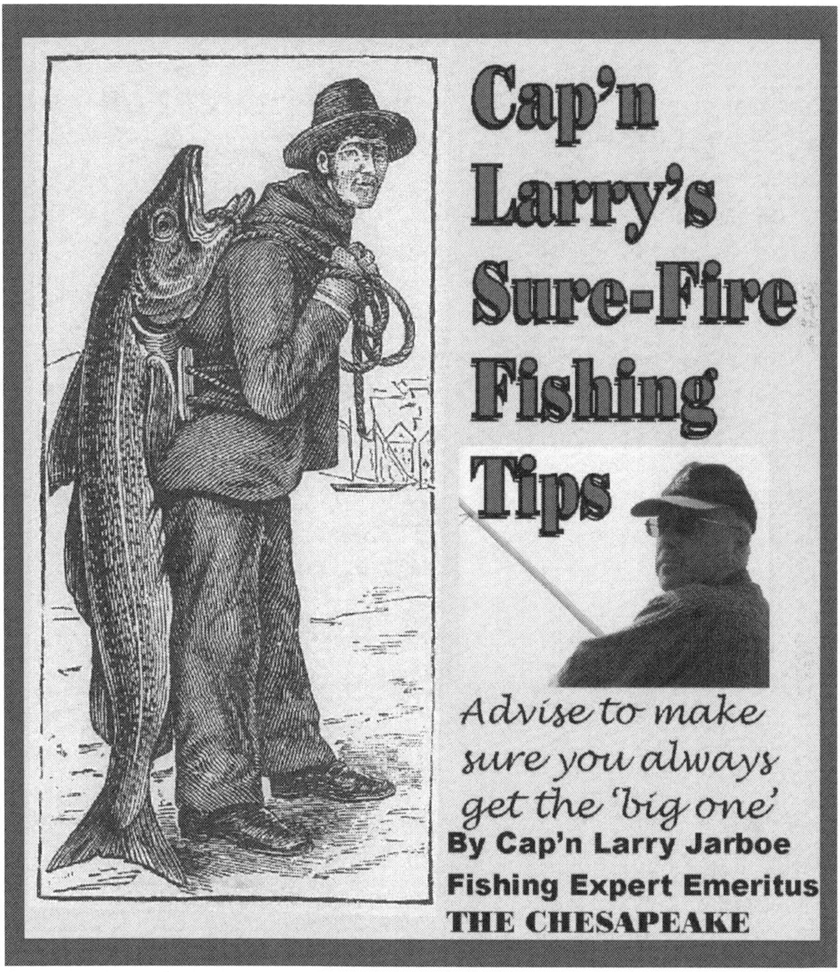
Cap'n Larry's Sure-Fire Fishing Tips
Advise to make sure you always get the 'big one'
By Cap'n Larry Jarboe
Fishing Expert Emeritus
THE CHESAPEAKE

Have you ever heard the term "bucket fisherman"?

Quite a few years ago, commercial fishermen in Florida labeled recreational fishermen who sold their five-gallon bucket of fish to restaurants or fish houses as bucket fishermen.

The name was no term of endearment as the full-time fishermen resented the competition from the larger network of fishermen, most of which were retired codgers simply looking to offset some of their fishing and boating expenses.

Today, the competition does not exist to any great extent as a commercial license is needed to sell most species of fish that have major value. Essentially, the Federal and State governments have put the little bucket fisherman out of business.

It happened very gradually. First, a law was passed that required fishermen to get a commercial license to catch snapper and grouper beyond recreational limits and legally sell their fish.

That was not too bad.

The license was available to all who applied and paid twenty-five bucks. That actually made the bucket fishermen official registered commercial fishermen.

Then, the State of Florida or the Feds required yearly sales of five thousand dollars to keep the license which knocked most of the little guys out. Later, they capped the number of licenses sold. Today, you have to buy two snapper/grouper licenses directly from the commercial fishermen, retire one license and fish the other. Figure on paying twenty grand for the right to legally sell your bucket of fish.

Bucket fishermen have become a thing of the past.

However, the most important commodity that you carry on your boat is still a bucket.

Naturally, you can carry your gear on board with that plastic bucket. While fishing, I throw a block of ice in a half bucket of water to keep my pan fish cool and calmed down before transferring them to the cooler. A bucket can also be used in a gastrointestinal emergency as a marine head (toilet). That is certainly not the bucket you should keep your fish in.

The most important function of a bucket on a boat is the one, hopefully, none of us will need. The best bilge pump is a scared boater with a bucket.

About twenty years ago, I ran an oyster diving charter for Captain Ken Pumphrey on his wooden lapstreak cabin cruiser out of Chesapeake Beach. The morning was flat calm, but a dense fog set in as we were cruising to Holland Point Bar.

Tourists travel by water taxi at Annapolis harbor. *THE CHESAPEAKE photo*

Fortunately, I had made a prior run and had course, R.P.M. and time numbers so I was able to put the three numbers together to put us right over the very large oyster bar. This was long before G.P.S units were readily available. I instructed the divers to stay close to the boat and listen close to home in on the bell that would be ringing every minute if they should get out of visual range.

As the mate was culling oysters that the divers brought back to the boat, I rang the bell every minute and listened intently for any other vessels cruising through the fog. I was deeply involved in the process of ringing the bell and focusing on the divers in the water and avoiding a potential collision with another boat when a lady diver came aboard. She was finished with her dive.

She asked where she might change out of her wetsuit into warm clothes. I directed her to the cabin where she closed the door and went below.

When she came up, she commented to me, "There's a lot of water down there."

It's pretty hard to look calm and move like lightning, but that was my intent as I slid down the steps into the cabin. Sure enough, there was a lot of water slopping around in the bilge threatening to cover the floorboards.

Morris Point Inn off of St. Clements Bay is a popular eatery accessible by land or water. *THE CHESAPEAKE photo*

I pulled up the floorboard over the forward bilge pump. As they so often do, the floating automatic pump switch had failed. Fortunately, Capt. Ken's manual over-ride switch worked and the pump started humming and pumping. I pulled loose another floorboard and grabbed a five-gallon bucket to assist the pump.

As I moved back and forth out of the cabin with a full bucket of water to toss overboard ringing the bell on each trip, the mate who was still culling oysters asked if he could help.

"No, the water's going down. No sense for panic, yet." I told him.

When Capt. Ken called me to run the trip for him, he did mention that there was caulking cotton in the top drawer below the cabinets on the port side. That should have been a big hint to me on the condition of his boat which was called "Patches" which should have been a bigger clue.

When the bare wood of the bilge came into view, there was a strong flowing leak between two of the lapstreak planks on the bottom. The first caulking I shoved in with a flat bladed scraper actually went through the hull. I pushed in a bigger wad which stuck and packed more around it. The leak almost stopped.

When all the divers returned to the boat, the fog had still not dissipated. With the same time and R.P.M. numbers and the course reversed by 180 degrees, I headed for #2 marker of the Chesapeake Beach Channel. At the given time, I shut the boat down and navigated a few tight circles before anchoring the boat up.

Number Two marker could not be seen and the other channel markers would be impossible to see. Chesapeake Beach Channel is a hard bottom cut. Either side is shallow water where you will be aground.

About an hour later, the fog lifted. The #2 marker was a stone's throw down the river and the other channel markers were easy to see. After easing the boat into the slip, the mate and I enjoyed a hearty lunch in Chesapeake Beach with the divers before I dropped off the boat's keys to Capt. Ken at his dive shop in Huntington.

"Ken, you'd better put that boat in dry dock before running another charter," I advised him.

Capt. Ken took my advice and I took my leave of running oyster dive charters.

Always take a bucket with you when you go out on the water. That is the best advice I can give you.

Piney Point Lighthouse was the summer resort of Presidents in the early 1800's. Located on the Potomac River, the lighthouse now is open to the public. *THE CHESAPEAKE photo*

CHAPTER 34
A VISIT FROM ISABEL TO FITZIE'S

By Ken Rossignol
The Chesapeake

Fitzie's Restaurant and Marina, one of the many family operated seafood houses in Southern Maryland is now into its eighth season since the devastation of Hurricane Isabel.

Long known as Delahay's Marina, which was once a simple shucking house, bar and workboat marina, Fitzie's Restaurant and Marina is a well built and attractive waterfront dining spot located on Breton Bay.

With a view clear to the Commonwealth of Virginia, Fitzie's caters to families for great Southern Maryland cooking.

Fitzie's Marina, open Thursday thru Sunday, most of the year, also is one of the few places on the St. Mary's shoreline to have gas docks. ***THE CHESAPEAKE photo***

With Pam and Danny FitzGerald serving up their own recipe of homemade crabcakes, fresh pan-fried or broiled rockfish, large steamed shrimp and a great variety of other dishes, it's a good bet that one of the FitzGerald clan will be bringing your meal to your table, serving up the great breakfast or back in the kitchen peeling potatoes or washing dishes.

With Dan and Pam, it's been a family affair since they first bought the marina in 1993.

While Dan has long run a mortgage company and operated a construction crew for building custom homes, the front and center livelihood for his family quickly became the restaurant.

With a flock of FitzGerald's to back him up, three kids of his own and a dozen or so nieces and nephews rotating in and out of his nearby home on St. Clements Bay and in the restaurant, help is always nearby when a boat or van arrives with a large group of customers.

When Isabel struck in 2003, the FitzGerald's had spent 10 years working to build, renovate, modernize and expand their business to meet the demands of their customers for a good neighborhood seafood house on the Potomac.

Tucked away in a side creek off of Breton Bay, Fitzie's location would normally be considered a 'hurricane hole' as a protected cove.

Isabel had other ideas.

The storm came up through Virginia and did odd things to the region, ripping up normally secure and safe harbors and leaving alone exposed stretches of shoreline.

About noon on Sept. 18, 2003, Isabel was a serious storm. The weather radar and tv stations had tracked its progress of death and destruction as she hit the Atlantic Coast and now the first storm since the 1930's to make a path of turmoil and tragedy into the area was making a direct run for Southern Maryland.

As the wind howled and the debris began to fly through the area, the next big event, storm surge, began to drive up the water level. The wind pushed the water level up about a foot every half hour until the water was a full nine feet above its normal point.

For Fitzie's this meant it was wiped out.

High water is one thing, high water being driven by 90 mph winds is quite another.

The wind blew the surf right through the building, making live crabs and fish swim where cooked ones were once served on a daily basis.

The entire point was under water and up and down both shores of Breton Bay the homes and boats were devastated.

For the FitzGerald family, the task of building their dream had started again.

Dan Fitzgerald did over the next six months what he had done for ten years. He and his family dug in and rebuilt. What had been a shell of shattered dreams soon became a blueprint for building as Dan led the effort.

A complete overhaul of the place led to a new day for Fitzie's, a restaurant which sprang from dreams to reality in record time.

With a large family room on the second floor, complete with large windows overlooking the water and fireplace, the FitzGerald family can be right at home after a long day's business.

Never far from the business, with his home right around the corner, Dan can quickly meet with folks planning events even when the restaurant is closed. With Monday and Tuesday down days, it's still business as usual for Dan and Pam, who use the two days wisely, ordering food and doing advance food preparation.

In this photo, the water from Hurricane Isabel in 2003 had not yet receded.

CHAPTER 35
DRIFT INN KEEPS LEONARD COPSEY SPRY AT 92

By Ken Rossignol
The Chesapeake

DRIFT INN on the PATUXENT RIVER --- In 1939, Adolph Hitler had just invaded Poland and was marching across Europe.

President Franklin Delano Roosevelt was attempting anything to try to pull America out of the Great Depression while the Lend-Lease program was ramping up American production of tanks, planes and ships to send to Britain and Russia to use against the Nazis as the U. S. tried to stay out of the war.

During that year, Maryland was still producing record bounties of crabs and oysters and the Patuxent River was still one of the principal harvesting grounds of both.

It was that year, in December, on Friday the 13th of, which Josephine and Leonard Copsey got married at St. Joseph's Catholic Church in Morganza.

Leonard said he wasn't superstitious and the priest said that damn if he was either, so they got hitched up. Leonard still chuckles today to recall the words of the priest. Leonard was 20, Josephine was 18 and the world was their oyster...and crab...and clam.

It was the year before that the Gov. Harry W. Nice Bridge which carries Rt. 301 across the Potomac River to Virginia opened for traffic that the Copsey's began their quest to farm, run the Granddaddy of all Maryland crab houses, raise kids and live a long and wonderful life.

The Copsey's Drift Inn has been the lynch-pin for three other seafood restaurants and outlets in the area. Daughter Sissy and her family run the

Sandgates Inn; son 'Lonnie-Boy' and his wife Elaine run Captain Leonard's Crabhouse, while daughter Peewee and her husband Ralph Gray run Leonard Copsey's Seafood Market while the Drift Inn is now operated by his daughter Punkin and her husband, Jerry Bowles.

The first lesson the Copsey's taught their children was to work hard. Next in line were to cook fresh food good, always with generous portions and then to treat their customers great. It's a simple philosophy and has worked well for decades.

Leonard Copsey's adventures with formal education intertwined with the lessons of life and before achieving stellar success in academia, he provided space for others in the school house and went out to find his fortune on the water.

With a large oyster shucking house next to his crab house, Leonard soon was trucking oysters all over the East Coast in cans branded with the name of Drift Inn.

With crab pickers, oyster shuckers and watermen coming and going with their catches, Drift Inn was a center of commerce on the Patuxent River and the Copsey's were at the right in the middle of it all.

City folks would find their way down to the river, Calvert residents would come by boat and local people would motor over from Leonardtown, Avenue and Budds Creek for crabs on the weekends.

Slot machines got a work out while trays of crabs were carried out to long tables covered in brown paper with hungry crustacean devouring customers crowded round.

Spiced shrimp, soft shell crabs, crab balls, fried shrimp, fresh fish and hush puppies have also been sold by the tons over the years in the old crab house, along with plenty of pitchers of beer.

Never has a politician running for Governor of Maryland in the last 60 years failed to make a visit to Drift Inn and go from table to table shaking hands with folks up to their elbows in crab mustard.

In 2009, former Congressman and present Senator Roy Dyson was on hand to congratulate the Copsey's on their important dates as Punkin, Jerry, and Miss PJ Bowles threw a surprise birthday party for Leonard.

The life story of the success of the Copsey family mirrors the story of America in that hard work produces rewards. While the American family has been content to allow a big part of the family to sit on their cans and collect rewards taken by force from those who do work, in the Copsey family, no one sits on their cans with their hand out. They all work. At an early age, the youngest are assigned tasks at cleaning tables or peeling shrimp, but there is no free ride for anyone. This is a lesson that America needs to return to as the Marxist-in-Chief in the White House attempts to spread the wealth around.

When crabs get scarce, Leonard Copsey doesn't put a closed sign on his crab house door or tell folks that he is out of crabs. Instead, he gets up at 2 am and drives to the Eastern Shore and brings back a truckload of crabs to keep his customers coming in the door.

At the birthday party thrown for Leonard, friends, family and longtime customers packed the closed up crab house which is open for business from April through October. One friend from Indian Head said that she and her husband come every weekend to Drift Inn and every time they have ordered a dozen crabs there were more than a dozen on the platter.

Giving folks more than what they bargain for, and keeping the promise of good food and good service has built a solid business over the years for the Copsey's and Josephine and Leonard Copsey have contributed their children, all hard workers, to America to help this nation prosper and grow.

The Patuxent River did a special delivery of crabs to the Drift Inn with Hurricane Isabel in 2003.

CHAPTER 36
PAT WOODBURN: PATRIOT HITS FINAL NOTE

By Ken Rossignol
The Chesapeake

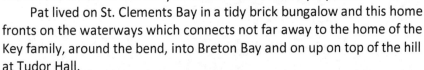

COMPTON --- The pomp and ceremony wasn't reserved by Pat Woodburn only for her famous renditions of The Star Spangled Banner, but that was what she was perhaps best known for by thousands.

This very traditional lady, who was also complicated and unorthodox, was connected to one of the early heroes of this nation by a poem.

Pat lived on St. Clements Bay in a tidy brick bungalow and this home fronts on the waterways which connects not far away to the home of the Key family, around the bend, into Breton Bay and on up on top of the hill at Tudor Hall.

Pat Woodburn and Francis Scott Key's family homes were just a few miles away, but their destinies were separated by nearly 200 years.

One was a singer, the other a writer, but they shared a song.

A son of the Key family, Francis was a lawyer in Washington at the time that the British brought war again to the United States in 1814 and when they marched on Washington and burnt our Capitol and the White House, their commander seized an Upper Marlboro farmer as a prisoner and took him away with their fleet as they sailed down the Patuxent and headed to Baltimore to lay waste to that city.

Francis Scott Key was close friends with the Upper Marlboro citizen and obtained permission from President James Madison to arrange an exchange of prisoners in order to free his friend.

Key was allowed by the British to conduct this trade but made to wait until they finished their siege of Fort McHenry.

As the night wore on, Key pulled out a pen and wrote a poem on the back of an envelope, telling the story of the explosive events of the night and the resulting banner still waving in the morning light.

The poem was rushed to shore and soon the words were being sung.

From sea to shining sea this anthem has been embraced but few have taken this National Anthem to heart the way Pat Woodburn did.

Her intensity of summoning up each note and every word from deep within her bosom and projecting them all in perfect harmony gave Old Glory life in a way which seldom was matched.

Pat Woodburn's singing of the Star Spangled Banner will forever wave in the memories of those whom she stirred with her exciting rendition.

Pat took her song seriously and likely her life ended with that song when she sang at a hospital fundraiser.

To the end of her days, Pat was a Democrat, but one who seriously questioned the strange paths being followed by the national party and it highest officials.

Her consternation over the health care proposals being bandied around by the Democrats had her furious to say the least.

While usually the top vote getter when she ran for Democratic Central Committee, proving she was more in synch with the average voter than the liberals who have come to dominate the local Democratic Party, she was less like the national members of her party all the time.

Had Pat not succumbed to a stroke, she quite possibly may have ended her life as a Republican. She had been close to the late Republican Senator Paul J. Bailey for many years and many of her friends had been leaving the Democrats in droves.

Pat was also close to Sen. Walter B. Dorsey and to Congressman and Senator Roy Dyson, who like her, are life-long conservative Democrats.

All elected officials in the area came under her scrutiny and had to answer her pointed questions. And they had better not patronize her.

Pat's values were traditional and conservative in many ways and she was deeply religious. She reached for more understanding of her faith in prayer groups and choirs, often attending Mass several times on Sundays.

While others may have trouble figuring out the world around them, it wasn't hard for Pat. Her world was as comfortable and dependable as the living room in which she often hosted her friends. She was a rock in an unstable world.

She was, at the end of her life, shaken to the core by the chicanery going on in Washington, which threatens the health care of senior citizens. Her sense of betrayal at the Democratic Party should make the sneakier leaders of the Democrats be glad she passed, for had she lived she would have become a beacon and leader of older folks standing up against the liberals.

Perhaps Pat's grounding in the illustrious words of Key's poem guided her all her life, certainly her stirring version of the National Anthem not only brought her many ovations but also educated folks about our nation's heroes defending Fort McHenry and defending America against invaders.

Certainly, America is at peril again with invaders attacking this nation from within and enemies threatening our shores and freedom around the world.

For a long while, we had Pat Woodburn to gird us, and now we must carry the forward the memory of her stalwart pride and boisterous enthusiasm of our national honor.

God Bless Pat and God Bless America!

This was the 1935 celebration of Maryland Day.
Photo courtesy of Cue Ball Raley.

CHAPTER 37
D-DAY VETERAN GIVES FIRST PERSON ACCOUNT OF LANDINGS ON OMAHA BEACH

By Ken Rossignol
The Chesapeake

LEXINGTON PARK --- Rastus "Smokey" Holcomb served on the USS Arkansas and participated in 13 convoys across the North Atlantic, several invasions in the European theater but the biggest military action of all time was the invasion of Normandy on D-Day, June 6, 1944.

The retired Navy veteran who joined the service in 1934 at the height of the depression also got married that year. But it was his service on the Arkansas on D-Day that will never leave his memory.

Asked if he ever thought that after the end of World War II that he would ever see American planes bombing Europe again, as has been underway for the past two months, Holcomb said the war was supposed to be the war that ended all wars.

"I never dreamed of it," said Holcomb. "I hope they won't send ground troops in there, we lost 9,000 in one day there at Normandy."

When did the crew of the Arkansas first learn that they were going to mount the invasion that everyone was waiting to come? That was the day for which both sides in the war had been preparing, that the Germans had massed an "Atlantic Wall" to repel and that the Allies had been assembling tens of thousands of men, planes and ships in England for the big day.

"About three days before the invasion," said Holcomb. "Eisenhower came aboard the ship and gave us a little speech and told us there was going to be the biggest invasion in the history of the world. It was, the most ships and men, there were a lot of ships from England and two French cruisers in there."

"We went in the night before, went across the English Channel and anchored 4,000 yards from the beach. No, we didn't get any sleep, there were three battleships, the Texas, the Nevada and the Arkansas."

"During the night the bombers were coming over from England bombing the beaches, you could see the antiaircraft fire, the bombers kept it up the whole night. One of our bombers was shot down and we could see it falling, some of the crew bailed out. You could see some of the people who bailed out in yellow life rafts."

"After daylight they opened fire on us and we opened fire back. We used our main battery; we had 12 twelve inch guns. This was one of the old battleships, we used armor piercing shells because the guns were 20 feet deep of reinforced concrete, we knew where all the gun emplacements were before we went in there because the planes had taken pictures of them, we had certain guns assigned to us on Omaha Beach, which was the rough one. We were anchored, we had orders that if we got hit we were going to slip the anchor, we kept the engines ready to go and we were going to run her aground and act as a fort, but we didn't have to, we didn't get hit."

"The landing craft went in alongside us, all kinds of landing crafts, those guys would wave to us as they went by, the transports anchored back of us, they didn't want them to get hit. They unloaded the landing craft off of them, the water was rough. We were scheduled to go in on the 5th, but they changed it because of the rough seas."

"I saw landing craft get hit when they got close to the beach, they took hits, you could see them when the dropped the front down, they were wading and swimming ashore, the backpacks was pretty heavy, if they didn't get in shallow enough water, certainly they would drown. Some of them got hit when they got in close. We sent a whale boat out for the bomber crew and picked them up, all three of them were wounded."

"Smaller craft picked up the wounded from the beach," said Holcomb.

"We watched all the paratroopers going in and bailing out. We stayed in there and bombarded as long as we could, we could only shoot so far after the Army advanced we couldn't shoot anymore without hitting our own men. So went back to Plymouth, England, a lot of ships did get hit. We were called back to Cherbourg, Gen. Hodges was bogged down and he asked for fire support from the Navy, and I saw the Texas get hit, and a cruiser and a destroyer got a hit."

The shelling got real close for the men of the Arkansas.

"We had 11 straddles over the Arkansas, some short, some over, big splashes; our planes were spotting for us. We were just there one day, the hit on the Texas had some casualties, on the destroyer, they hit the bridge, the signal gang on the navigation bridge, didn't sink them."

"They said there were at least 1,100 planes that went over that day, and some of the planes had 2 gliders with them loaded with paratroopers. You could see them jumping out, the shoots blossoming, anti-aircraft was so fierce they went in further.

"I was on an antiaircraft gun, a 40 mm, I was gun captain a Junkers 88 came in while it was dark, it dropped a bomb right down next to us, we all aimed at him, no ship got credit for it, because too many ships were shooting at it but he did get shot down.

"The destroyers were running up and down the beach, they had small guns aiming at little machine gun nests, there were cruiser running up and down, but these battleships were all anchored, there were three British battleships too, old ones, all of ours were old ones, ours was commissioned in 1912, they were expendable, we were acting as a fort. Nobody had to run them aground."

"They were going by us for hours, there was no end to it, they kept going in, but, of course, some of the barges got sunk."

"I had a classmate who was killed that day, a kid from Tellico Plains who went to high school with me, he was in the army. Berry was his name. It's been so long now, I forget his first name."

"We then made another invasion in southern France, before D-Day we were at Casablanca, we come back to Boston and put new guns on the ship, we wore the guns out on the Normandy beachhead, the liners get hot inside the guns and they stretch. We went through the canal, they had worked 7 days and 7 nights in Boston, they always made two sets of guns for a ship."

"Then we got to Long Beach, Pearl Harbor and out to rendezvous with a whole bunch of ships, with ten battleships and we went into Iwo Jima and we bombarded Iwo Jima, them people were in caves and everything over there, and they brought the landing craft the next day, the bombers came across, we laid off and let them bomb them, they would shake the old battleships out there in the harbor. We were 1200 yards from where they raised the flag, you could see the Marines going in there in waves, a bunch of them got killed, the next day or two, we stayed in there bombing things, when the Marines raised the flag on, the captain passed the word, we were close and watched them push the flag up, all rocks around it. One of the old Kingfishers got shot down and nobody survived, it was an observation plane, they spot for the guns, they get up above to guide us on how to knock out those gun emplacements, they got in too close."

"After that we went to Okinawa. We stayed down there for about 40 days and nights, that's where Ernie Powell was killed, the reporter. Just about every day we had kamikazes coming at us. We shot antiaircraft at them, but the trouble is that when you hit them they were on automatic pilot and dive right into the ship."

"One Sunday afternoon, there were 26 ships in the formation and the sky was full of kamikazes, all kinds of them, torpedo planes, they said that out of 26 ships, 13 were hit that day. Several came close to us, one of them came real close. We secured it out there and came back to Guam and had to go in dry-dock, and that is where I left the ship, came back and got transferred to duty, Mare Island, California for shore duty."

Smokey Holcomb came to Maryland after the war where he and family made their home.

"I got married to Nellie Lee in 1934 in Chatsworth, Georgia, we grew up together in Tennessee, she taught school in the Smokey Mountains, she graduated from the University of Tennessee, and she taught school for thirty some years while I was in the Navy, have one son, Jack, lives in Wildewood, worked on the base for 38 years, been married 65 years, have two grandchildren, Steve, he is an assistant attorney general of Maryland and his wife's an attorney also, Diane, works in Washington for a Judge; my other grandson, Chris Holcomb, is in Texas A & M, teaches English out there, both of those boys went to Ryken. We are 85 years old."

What does Smokey remember most about D-Day and watching out over the ocean as the battle got underway?

"I will always remember when daylight broke, the first German shell fell close to us, right off of our port bow, as soon as they fired, and we opened fire."

"I hope Americans appreciate the sacrifice that was made that day by those who died, there were a lot of deaths, the Army took the beating, a lot of sailors got killed that day. I had two brothers that went in the day after, the beach was pretty well secured, they went all the way to the Battle of the Bulge, they were in Patton's Army, they like to froze to death. One of them is still alive, he is about 81 or 82."

Smokey Holcomb was asked what he thought about the cutbacks for military funerals for America's veterans, substituting an honor guard and bugler who plays taps to one soldier with a flag and a tape recording to put in a portable stereo for graveside services.

"I think it is a shame, you can't say too much about it," said Holcomb. "I hate to say too much, we should give them something. They finally took care of me in Bethesda last year, so I can't bad mouth them too much, but they have taken away a lot of our privileges."

Has Smokey ever been back to Normandy to look around since the war or is he interested in going back?

"I have never been back to Normandy and I have no desire to go back there, just a big cemetery there, I guess, some of my shipmates went back there when they had the 50th," said Holcomb. "We have another reunion of our shipmates coming up this fall, in Myrtle Beach, at least a couple of hundred of us show up when we get together."

When you see Smokey Holcomb around town, thank him and his fellow veterans for doing their part in beating the Japanese and Germans and providing a better life for Americans.

(This interview was conducted in 1998. Smokey Holcomb is now deceased.)

Chapter 38
KAY DAUGHERTY: THE FIRST LADY OF LEXINGTON PARK

By Ken Rossignol
The Chesapeake

LEXINGTON PARK --- The long-time better half of the late John T. "Jack" Daugherty, Kay, died in 2006.

Kay and Jack came to Lexington Park when Jack was assigned to the Patuxent River Naval Air Station after he flew combat missions during WWII in the South Pacific. A Marine pilot, Jack, and Kay, a school teacher, became an important part of the social, economic, educational and political community from the mid-forties until the time of their deaths.

Teaching first at the old Great Mills Elementary School, Kay also raised the couple's two children while at the same time establishing herself as a quiet philanthropist involved in all manner of charities and church work.

Known for her care and concern for animals, Kay was not only a constant patron of animal welfare groups such as the Animal Welfare League and the Humane Society; she also regularly adopted dogs herself or fostered them in her home.

Katherine W. "Kay" Daugherty provided a lot of balance to her husband, an outgoing and boisterous businessman who not only actively participated in politics but even ran for the state senate himself in 1958.

Where Jack was a Democrat, Kay was a Republican, where Jack was at good and rough and tumble business and politics, Kay was demure, polite and genteel.

Where Jack prided himself on making money, Kay quietly gave it away as a patron of the arts, of local starving artists and musicians as well as keeping plenty of puppies in chow. Even with their children, they balanced life, turning out a teacher, Katie, and a lawyer, Tom.

While Jack started up the old Jack Daugherty's Merchandise Mart, the Esso station and later Maryland Bank & Trust, Kay taught school, raised the kids and put dinner on the table.

They both were essential parts of the great generation who won the war, got the kids to little league and found time to participate in every possible civic function important to the community.

They were devoted to their own grandchildren and always found it in their hearts and wallets to be generous to many other children in the community.

Where Jack would sputter and pick at his head while turning red when angered, Kay was the epitome of the level-headed, even-tempered lady always in control of her emotions and helping to keep others in control of theirs.

What they had in common was a love of St. Mary's County, where they pitched in to make it a better place to live, in every possible way.

Kay's name is on the plaque outside of the old library, as a trustee, for the fine brick building which the county's citizens and taxpayers built for the post-war boom town of Lexington Park in 1958, was just one of the ways she invested in the town and the county.

Many years and many donated dollars later, the Daugherty-Palmer Commons at St. Mary's College was named for her parents and for Jack's. Their names and their endowments have soared into the millions at the college as well as in Lexington Park with money from the couple going to their church and their community in countless public and private ways.

It was commonplace for Kay to be seen driving around with at least one dog in her station wagon and several bags of dog food as she went about her errands or picking up an old friend to take them to a doctor's appointment.

As the years began to take their toll on her body, they never defeated her spirit, her manners or her genuine kindness for everyone she met.

Where her late husband's passing left all knowing that the wake of his days will be rolling back and forth across the local waters for a long time, Kay's passing will only leave behind a sweet aroma of spring, touching the memories of many of us for years to come, each time we are able to say, we knew and miss Kay, the First Lady of Lexington Park.

Chapter 39 Marie Dyson Left Legacy of Faith & Family

By Ken Rossignol
The Chesapeake

GREAT MILLS — The matriarch of one of the largest families in St. Mary's County, Marie Dyson, died in 2006.

Marie came to St. Mary's County as a young woman to work as a telephone operator when the Patuxent River Naval Air Station was built in 1943. She rented a room at Great Mills from John Samuel Dyson and Florence Aud Dyson and soon met their son Leroy Dyson whom she married and together they raised eight children; J.C., Lee, Roy, Vi, Lynn, Mary Katherine, Steve, and Patricia.

With 16 grandchildren and one great-granddaughter, Marie never lost count and never stopped knowing their names or needs, finding time for all. Marie would include the date, day of the week, time of birth and birth weight on the birthday card she would send to each of her family and was able to recite these family stats on a moment's notice.

Marie was the chief telephone operator of the new central phone system that the Navy brought with them to St. Mary's County to replace the scattered kitchen operated system which had been in place, often putting placing phone calls behind making apple pies.

Marie came to St. Mary's from Salisbury where she had been raised by her parents, Royden Street Meise, and Gladys McFee Meise. She was one of six children and is survived by her sister Pat Banks of Salisbury and her brother Hugh Meise of Oklahoma.

In addition to taking care of her family, Marie was back and forth from her kitchen to the kitchens of others, bringing meals to those in need and driving others to doctor and church. With Leroy, Marie ran the Dyson Lumber Company until their children were old enough to join and take over the business.

Marie Dyson took the time to handwrite the words 'thank you' on each and every invoice she sent out every month, keeping the personal touch as her family's business grew over the years from being a simple saw mill selling some bolts and nails to a thriving building center.

Marie's dedication to her church, family and community extended to her significant role in politics, as she volunteered in and kept open the

Democratic Headquarters in 1974 at Millison Plaza and when her son Roy filed that year for Delegate, printed out her stuffed ham recipe and had it printed on a campaign card, making her contribution to politics legendary for good taste and spicy flavor.

From astronaut and Senator John Glenn, to Baltimore luminaries such as Teddy Venetoulis, Sen. Paul Sarbanes Gov. Harry Hughes and Governor William Donald Schaefer, the parade of politicians coming to Marie Dyson's kitchen and backyard campaign events were colorful but far outweighed by the thousands of folks who had never before been involved in politics but pushed Marie's son Roy far ahead in the polls as they gave their votes and cooked stuffed hams as well.

With television reporters on her lawn and an endless procession of friends and campaign workers in her kitchen and living room, Marie Dyson presided over a significant effort of family and friends who worked tirelessly in Congressman Roy Dyson's many campaign events, many of which were held in her backyard, with thousands attending to eat beef BBQ and listen to bands.

Whether she was presiding over a Field Day or taking a meal to a shut-in, Marie always had a kind word for everyone and knew which direction to take.

Marie had her finger on the pulse of the community, with the phone ringing endlessly; she also kept a TV tuned to CNN in her kitchen while the police scanner kept her informed of ambulance and fire calls, often the first notice that something might be wrong with friend or family.

Marie's own political work involved her long years of participation in the Democratic Club, local election campaigns and in 1992 was elected a Maryland presidential elector who cast a vote in the Electoral College.

In addition to being the mother of Senator Roy Dyson, her son-in-law, John Bohanan, is also an elected delegate from St. Mary's County. Her son Steve runs a hauling business, her children Vi, Lynn, Mary Katherine, Patricia, and JC run the family business while Lee recently retired from the United States Capitol Police.

Chapter 40
PRODUCTS THAT PROTECT THE CHESAPEAKE

By Cap'n Larry Jarboe
The Chesapeake

While cruising by car on a weekday lunch trip through Solomon's, I saw a boatload of happy anglers from the Miss Susie cleaning their catch. Each one had a trophy rockfish for a picture and fine family dining. Though today, a catch like this is a regular occurrence with professional charter captains like Capt. Greg Buckner, just a few years ago, there was a moratorium on catching rockfish due to the low population levels.

The recent limits on female crabs and the rebounding population figures for those clawed crustaceans show promise that effective natural resource regulations can help maintain sustainable, healthy fisheries. Hopefully, with an improved system of oyster sanctuaries, Maryland will achieve the perfect trifecta of common sense conservation regulations.

In the meantime, each of us also can play our part in protecting the Chesapeake Bay watershed that we live in.

This week, Duane Hendricks from Green Earth Solutions introduced me to a high-quality bio-degradable oil made from animal fat rather than petrochemicals. As a boater, the idea of a bio-degradable oil in a marine engine is critical to me. No matter how careful any of us might be, invariably, an inboard engine will leak some oil into the bilge. The very word bilge conjures up greasy, black water. Unlike the petroleum based oil, the G-oil does not pollute the water with a toxic residue.

The Green Motor Oil sold by Green Earth Solutions does cost more than regular motor oil, but you can go twice as far on an oil change. That saves the cost of a filter and the time saved by doing only half as many oil changes. The economic benefits are as good as the environmental benefits.

Today, I put G-oil changes into my marinized Ford 302 engine in my 20' Shamrock and the hand me down Toyota Camry with over 290,000 miles on the odometer. Not a single Arab sheik got a penny from the transaction and I will have more time to go fishing.

A pretty good deal for you, me and the Chesapeake. Check out Duane's line of bio-degradable products at: getgreenearthsolutions.com.

The Linda Carol works the Bay from Crisfield, Md. THE CHESAPEAKE TODAY photo

CHAPTER 41 **PREPARING TO PUT THE BOAT UP FOR WINTER**

By Cap'n Larry Jarboe

Fall is here, and winter is knocking on the door. For some boaters that means making preparations soon to put our vessels into hibernation until the chilly waters begin to warm again.

For others, this is the time of year we look forward to.

As we pass the summer time by bottom fishing, trot-lining or chumming, we eagerly look forward to the day when the weather cools enough to need a sweater and the water is too cold to jump in.

This is the start of the fall Rockfish season, and the colder it is, "The bigger they are".

For many fall fishermen, they tend to make several outings during summer, but don't ask much of their vessels until the frigid temperatures roll around. Cold morning start-ups, a hard run to your favorite spot, long hours of slow speed trolling and again a hard run home. You're asking a lot of your floating steed, so here are a few tips to help it run strong.

Many feel the engine/drive system is the most crucial part of your boat. I disagree, as if your drive-train quits, you can just float until help arrives. Number one on your pre-season checklist should be the hull itself since if it were to fail- you'd be wet and fighting hypothermia.

All thru-hulls should be well-sealed and should not be seeping any water. If you've got water running into your boat from anywhere, fix it.

That leads us to your bilge pump. If you're going to rely on something to potentially save your boat and life in the event of a hull breach or breaking waves, you should have the biggest one possible and two are even better, wired separately for redundancy.

Make sure all your required safety equipment is there but add some items due to the cold weather. Dry clothes, rain gear, a blanket, some snacks and potable water should be ever present during cold trips.

This can make the difference between and uncomfortable wait for help and a lifesaving or recovery mission. Never fish by yourself. If you fall in the water, the hypothermia clock starts ticking.

If you can't make it back into your boat, you're fish bait.

If you do make it back aboard- you will be in a race to get home before your motor-skills give out. Let your buddies know where you'll be going. That way if you do run in trouble, help will have a much easier job finding you. Plan on having a catastrophic incident every time you get on your frost covered boat.

Better to have something and not need it than need it and not have it! Have your batteries tested free at a local auto parts store, and replace if necessary. Batteries work harder than ever in colder temperatures and you don't want to ruin a great trip with a borderline battery.

Grab a drink and a screwdriver and check all the fasteners you can get to.

Bow rails, windshields, seats and other items loosen up over time, and with the pounding your boat can get in rough fall waters, you don't want pieces falling off.

Make sure your drive system is running well.

It's not a bad idea to have your mechanic look it over.

If you're inclined to tackle this yourself- check all your fluids, replace your fuel-water separator filter, and grease anything that moves with some white lithium grease.

Always run a marine fuel stabilizer such as STABIL Marine. This will help your fuel system stay fresh and avoid long-term problems. Also avoid fuel with high ethanol content as marine fuel system components hate it.

Last- If you trailer your boat, it needs a quick once over as well.

Your boat may be 100 percent, but it won't do you any good if you can't move it to the ramp!

Check your lights, if any need replacing use the newer LED style. They cost a little more but are well worth the investment. If you're going to troubleshoot your own lighting problems, make sure all connections are made with marine style butt connectors that incorporate heat-shrink.

Get them at Lowes or Wal-Mart, as they are the same ones at marine stores but for a fraction of the price. Check your winch cable and lubricate the winch. Jack up your trailer and shake your wheels/tires. If they feel like they have some play between them and your axle your bearings may need to be checked.

Check them for wear and for proper inflation. If you have bearing buddies on your hubs, grease them with waterproof grease until you see the grease fitting start to move out.

Hopefully, these tips will keep your boat from any downtime, and keep those rod tips jumping. Be safe, have fun and send in any boating related questions and we will be glad to answer them in future issues.

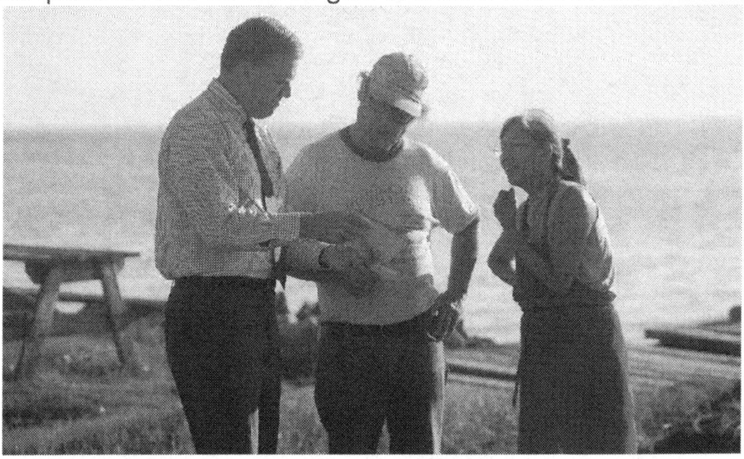

Senior aide to Congressman Steny Hoyer, John Bohanan assists the owners of Courtney's campground after Hurricane Isabel hit their property hard in 2003.
THE CHESAPEAKE photo

The McKay & Bohanan Store in Park Hall, Md., was operated by Bohanan's family. *Photo courtesy of Mayor J. Harry Norris III.*

A young Osprey chick awaits a meal. THE CHESAPEAKE TODAY photo

This family strolls out onto the Bill Burton State Park Fishing Pier, which is the old span of the Rt. 50 Bridge over the Choptank River at Cambridge, Md.
THE CHESAPEAKE TODAY photo

CHAPTER 42
STIHL AFLOAT

The absolutely most unbelievable fishing adventure in my memory began with a trip up Indian Creek to clear away a Loblolly pine tree that had fallen across the creek.

Indian Creek is a tributary of The Patuxent River. It is also the border between St. Mary's and Charles Counties. This creek provides a lovely excursion trip that transitions from salt marsh habitat to hardwood forest. There is also some fine perch fishing where the creek narrows in the hardwood forest.

Some years ago, I took my 17' Grumman canoe with an electric trolling motor up the creek to catch a bucket of white perch in the honey hole beside the clay bank. I had dipped a butter tub full of fresh grass shrimp from the nearby shore grass. Those little buggers are the best bait

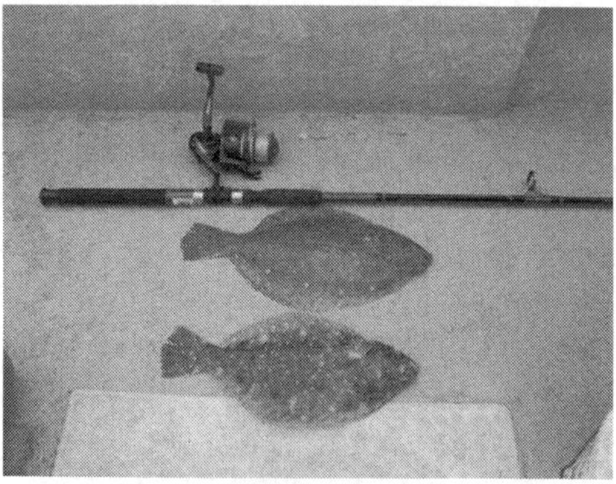

to hook a stringer of perch. Unfortunately, the spring rains had loosened the roots of an old red heart pine that had fallen across the creek blocking my course to the hot spot.

So, I fished the waters downstream. Caught far fewer fish than I should have. And, resolved to deal with the wooden barricade.

A week later, after consulting the tide tables, I grabbed two Stihl chainsaws from the mill and recruited my fishing buddy and left handed guitar picker, Ralph Long, to help clear that snag in the creek.

I eased the 25' KenCraft gingerly up the creek during the top end of the incoming tide. I carefully worked the boat around and put my plow anchor overboard far ahead of the fallen tree. Then, I fed out line as the tide pulled the boat to the tree. When the dive platform at the stern of the boat came a few inches from the tree, I hitched off the line.

I marked the log with a blue lumber crayon to cut enough space so that I could squeeze my canoe through, but a larger boat couldn't get through. Ralph and I went to work. Both Stihl saws cranked on the first pull. Being left handed, Ralph stood on the starboard side of the dive platform straddling the big gap the big hammerhead shark had consumed during the past short winter trip to Florida.

We wound up those razor sharp saws and bore down on each blue mark in front of us. In no time at all, a big block of pine dropped into the water and floated up the creek. The way was then clear for me and my canoe. Your skiff would get stuck.

We pulled up the plow anchor and eased out the creek. It was early summer, so, rock, perch, spot, and catfish (croaker were virtually non-existent back then) should be swarming upon Buzzard Island Bar on the Calvert County side of the Pax River channel.

At the top edge of the bar, I slipped the plow anchor overboard. I should note here that I am a precision anchoring fanatic. Good fishing spots are often only a few feet across. You're either on the hole or off. That is the difference between fishing and catching.

I also made a point to keep a sharp point at the end of my plow anchor that was hollow ground with a little Makita grinder. This design anchor will quickly grab and set in sand, grass, mud, and oyster bottom. A couple feet above the stainless anchor chain on the anchor line there was a snap clip with a very special fish attracting purpose.

To this spring loaded clip, I attached a big mesh bag with a frozen block of ground up fish carcasses recycled from past fishing trips. As the chum thawed, bits of fish meat treats would spread across the bottom concentrating feeding fish directly under the boat.

So, with the anchor and chum bag overboard and about fifty feet of line paid out, Ralph and I awaited the onset of the moving ebb tide.

During slack tide, we did not expect to catch much more than bar dogs (a.k.a. toadfish). We broke out the Lance Toastchee crackers that had become our regular fishing survival food. While we were munching on those peanut butter crackers, the bow of the KenCraft moved quickly around. We started moving downriver.

Nothing in my past experience had prepared me for having the bottom of the river drag my boat downriver. The anchor line was taught and singing through the water as we were pulled at a steady six or seven knots toward the Bay.

The physical impossibility of moving bottom finally registered in my uncomprehending mind. A greater realization occurred. Something, a very big something, was dragging us down the river.

"Ralph, we caught a big one!" I said and pointed to the anchor line.

I swung the boat back and forth to offer more resistance to feel out just what kind of creature or submarine we were hooked to. After about the fourth cycle, a huge manta ray flew out of the water on a very short leash. The plow anchor was embedded in the beast's upper gaping jaw. That monster must have tried to eat the chum bag. The momentum of its great body had snagged the 700 ought hook, otherwise known as a plow anchor, in its gaping mouth.

Seeing a giant manta ray with a twenty-five foot wingspread doing acrobatics off the bow of your boat is like having a stealth bomber buzz you at low altitude. Ralph and I knew what a manta ray looked like as the renowned local bass player and acupuncturist, Big George Henderson, had caught and released a very small one on a past Keys fishing trip with us. Those aerial maneuvers were awe inspiring. What we were witnessing was just plain terrifying!

After a couple minutes (it seemed like two hours) of trying to shake that plow anchor hook, the devil ray decided to run to the Bay.

From L to R: Chris Long, Sandi Tucker, and George Hall

Again, at steady six or seven knots we headed past Senator Paul Bailey's waterfront farm, Drift Inn, Sandgates Inn, Seabreeze, and down the Patuxent River. I steadily worked the wheel back and forth attempting to tire the massive creature.

Ralph took over the wheel as I went up to the bow to put a little distance between us and that monster manta ray. I pulled a big coil of line up on the deck and tried to slip the line past the anchor cleat. The intense pressure of three tons of stress had locked the line hard down on the cleat. Until the line might go slack, the hitched line would not be worked loose. I took over the wheel as we continued our ride down the Patuxent.

Cruising past Greenwell Manor, Hollywood Shores, and the old Jones Wharf public landing, I had time to think about the enormity of capturing such a big fish.

"Ralph, we're going to be famous. No one in the history of Southern Maryland has ever caught such a big fish. They're going to frame the picture at the Tackle Box." I said.

"Yep, and you're going to have one heck of a taxidermist bill," Ralph replied.

Leave it to Ralph to spoil a good day.

So we cruised back and forth as the ray passed Drum Cliffs and Clarkes Landing. Off the end of Myrtle Point, the manta stopped and the line went slack.

Ralph and I looked over each side to see a massive black body arise directly beneath the boat. Each wing broke the water and circled together above us.

The great canopy of fish flesh inspired Ralph to call out, "We don't got him. He's got us!"

One roll of that ray and we were done for.

"The chainsaws, Ralph!" I blurted.

We each grabbed a chainsaw from under the wide gunnels. Again, both Stihl saws started on the first pull. With a swift motion, each of us sliced through the wing on our respective sides of the boat. Plop, both wing tips fell on the gunnels with the tips crossed over the engine box.

From L to R: Gracie, Evan, Gracen, Quinn, & Ridgely

Neither of us had time to consider the lifetime supply of deep sea scallops behind us as the wounded ray dove straight down into the hundred foot plus depths that sweep past Myrtle Point. The boat stern popped up in the air like a pencil bobber. Ralph and I found our faces jammed into the windshield looking down at the water as the two giant severed wing tips slid past us into the river.

The boat recovered easily from the quick tug. Then, the ray exerted a more steady pull. The stern of the KenCraft arose again vertically and the bow went under water. The cabin reached about two-thirds under when the ray eased up.

The boat resumed her horizontal position.

"Ralph, one more pull and we're going down," I said. "If the cabin goes under, we'll sink like a rock."

I grabbed a Stihl chainsaw and jumped back up on the bow. With my left foot deep within the coil of anchor line on the bow and my right foot pushed against the anchor cleat, I had a slip-proof stance when the slow, insistent pull started.

As the bow started to go down, I pulled on the chainsaw starting cord. It did not fire. Quickly, I cranked again. No start on that pull. By the third pull, my feet were getting wet. I looked up the see Ralph's eyes as big as saucers with his face pressed against the windshield.

I was standing with the boat almost vertical against my left side. The anchor line slid forward and wrapped around my left leg while the bulk of my weight was supported by my right foot on the anchor cleat. As the water reached under my knees, I realized that I had forgotten something.

I forgot to flip the kill switch on the chainsaw.

A fast flip of the toggle switch and three more super quick pulls to clear the flooded carburetor and the saw started. The river was now flowing above my knees. The saw bar barely reached the taut line underwater without drowning the engine. I cut the line just past the anchor cleat nicking the gel coat in the process.

The boat slammed down to the river's surface knocking me to the top of the cabin. I untangled my left leg and got back into the cockpit.

The big one got away with my plow anchor, anchor chain, chum bag, and fifty feet of anchor line trailing behind.

That was the last time Ralph went fishing with me.

Chapter 43 Top Three Finest Fishing Piers in So. Maryland

By Cap'n Larry Jarboe
The Chesapeake

A few years ago, the "Hooked on Fishing" youth program hosted an all-day fishing derby at the Point Lookout State Fishing Pier in May. Though the camaraderie and picnic were wonderful, the kids only landed a couple fish.

I recommended to the Community Services Director, who hosted the drug intervention event that the months of June through the Fall would be a better time to catch fish off this pier. At the next year's event, in early June, dozens of fish were caught, measured, photographed and released. The kids got lots of prizes for the biggest, smallest, most, and most unusual fish. Hopefully, with the knowledge of a great healthy recreational activity available all around us in Southern Maryland, these kids will choose to get high on fishing rather than drugs or alcohol.

Catching fish from our public piers in May is a challenge as most piers are in relatively shallow water while the migratory fish are elsewhere. The rockfish and perch are still out in the channels waiting for the shallows to warm up.

There are three excellent piers to fish in May that are all on the Wicomico River. Bushwood Wharf, Chaptico Wharf, and Wicomico Shores Pier are excellent places to hook up on the jumbo croaker (a.k.a. hardhead) that make a spring migration up this river.

The best place to start in early May is Bushwood Wharf. Quade's Store is right beside this historic steamboat landing and wharf that has an adjacent boat ramp. The late Mrs. Quade and now, with her passing in 2010, her son George shared incredible memories of two lifetimes on the Potomac and Wicomico Rivers. They will also give you a daily catch report along with Mrs. Quade's internationally famous crabcake sandwich still available. In addition, they carry a good selection of the tackle needed to catch the local fish.

Further up the Wicomico River, Chaptico Wharf is a good bet as May progresses and those big croaker over sixteen inches long move upriver. This is another historic steamboat landing, wharf, and boat ramp, but there are no public facilities beyond a parking lot, porta-potty, and a trash can. So, make sure you bring your bait, tackle, soda, and a sandwich before you hit the pier.

After Mid-May, the Wicomico Shores Pier is a good bet to fling out a line for those big hardheads as well as picking up big channel catfish that are prowling for a meal. This is a pier rather than a wharf. It was built about fifty years ago as part of the Wicomico Shores Aviation and Yacht Club. The pier was built, the landing strip never materialized, and the development scheme went bust. Such a large facility with excellent showers and restrooms seems out of place at the end of Aviation Yacht Club Drive but it is a public facility available to the neighborhood and fishermen wanting to catch a stringer of fish or later in the season, a basket of crabs. There is also a new boat ramp for the more affluent boating fisherman.

Catching croaker, perch, catfish, and an occasional rockfish from these wharves and pier works best with a spinning rod capable of flinging a double hook bottom rig a long distance. An ounce or two drop sinker clipped to the bottom of the spreader rig is enough to hold bottom. 1/0 hooks are about the right size though I often use smaller when I have a hard time hooking up the nibblers.

Most important of all is good fresh bait. Live soft crabs are showing up in the local seafood stores. Cut fresh soft crab will catch almost any fish that swims in the salty side of the Chesapeake Bay watershed. One hook baited with soft crab and the other baited with table quality frozen squid cut in strips is a good one combo to hook up on big croaker or other fish swimming by in May.

A croaker bites somewhat aggressively and one sharp, hard set of the hook is enough to drive the point home. Then, hang on! Though croaker are considered panfish, pound for pound, they fight much better than many game fish. If the common Atlantic Croaker grew as big as a trophy Striped Bass, the croaker would be the most sought after fish on the East Coast. Expect to have a ball on 12 lb. class light tackle.

The flakey white meat fillets fried in a crispy batter are just plain delicious.

Might you expect to catch some good eating fish for dinner this month? Yes, you may.

Rock Hall, Md., boasts a great public beach. THE CHESAPEAKE TODAY photo

Picnic table is a great place to sort crabs on a workboat at Rock Hall, Md. THE CHESAPEAKE TODAY photo

Chapter 44 A Blossom in a Pine Tree

By Vi Englund
The Chesapeake

A door had closed in my life. One morning I awakened at dawn: I lingered by that closed door. Then, as in previous losses, I walked alone.

The wet grass beneath my feet healed my body. The trees overhead fed my spirit. And I kept hearing or thought I heard: Live it now. Live it now. You cannot live tomorrow unless you live today – this moment.

Then I became aware of the great process of time. We hold nothing. All things go. I became part of that stream of time when the ancient life-forms started. I could see those life-forms as though in progression. Vivid as a chart on a museum wall. Yet the ancient oaks speak only of today. An unbelievable optimism overflowed me. The Life-Force moves. It continues to grow and change. It re-creates from decaying hearts new grasses – perhaps in a different form. And there is an expanding consciousness to perceive the wonder of this movement of Life!

Suddenly I knew my part in this. It is not to war with progress. Not to spend my force grieving because the buffalo are gone and the whale may be leaving. Not grasping for some utopian future. But from my thought and feeling first in mind and heart and then in words, tell what it is – just what it is this day.

So, this day I saw a crimson blossom of a trumpet flower in a pine tree. It bloomed above fist-sized cones. I saw the arched head of a deer; the gentle grace of a doe in movement. I saw a cottontail, poised as a statue. For a while, I walked in the tracks of a raccoon. I sat on a moss-covered stump and wondered, what myth am I living? Promptly the answer came: Emerson's woodlot myth, I smiled. I thought I heard the chuckle of a friend.

I departed the woods and went to the beach. Through cracks in the pier, three inches from my eyes, I saw two barn swallows with their golden lined beaks closed. In their carefully feathered nest, they slept the deep sleep of infants' sleep. Their elders sat on the dock rail. They chatted together before starting the day of feeding their young. I heard the quack of a blue heron, and the plop of the dive of a tern. I listened to all the birds and did not care about their names.

Today I walked in the good earth. I felt a gnarled oak with these fingers. I saw a blossom in a pine tree, and it healed me. I said, "Let the past go. Let the future be. It is enough to feel, and see, and be in this instant in time."

I understood that the door was not really closed. All the life and live I'd known walked with me beneath the trees. Life flows in an endless stream. Being a part of life, we flow with it.

The swallows gather food
for their young.

I gather a
different food,
for a
different young.

Chapter 45 Meeting Great-Grandfather

By Joey Greenwell
The Chesapeake

Recently I allowed my five-year-old son to tag along on an afternoon squirrel hunt where he met his great grandfather.

The day we picked was windy and cold, almost too cold for his little body to stay warm. Little Joey was bundled up with so many layers he looked like "Ralphy" from the movie "A Christmas Story".

He waddled back and forth as we headed into the woods looking for a dry log to sit on and wait.

Once we picked a spot, we sat down and I reiterated to Little Joey how being still and quiet was the only way we would see a squirrel.

I knew it wasn't going to be long before he would tire of being still and the cold would seep through all his layers. It took about 20 minutes and he was ready to move about. We decided to some "run and gun" hunting.

This is the best way to introduce a little one to hunting; we just walk around the woods hoping to tree a squirrel before shooting it down.

The time passes by quicker for them and they stay warmer. Even if they don't see any squirrels, they have a good time walking around. After about an hour of walking the woods and seeing nothing, we decided to take a break. Little Joey helped me build a small fire and we sat around it to thaw ourselves a bit. While sitting there, Little Joey asked about the gun we were using.

I had brought out an old Winchester Model 24 side by side double barrel in 20 gauge.

As any 5-year-old will, he asked countless questions about this gun. As he regularly helps me clean my other guns, he was unusually interested in this one as he had never seen it before.

We talked about many things I knew about this gun and realized some things I had never noticed before. It is over 70 years old and is in remarkable shape for being so old.

My Great Grand Father was Dr. Charles Greenwell from here in St. Mary's County and his attention to detail showed in how well taken care of this weapon was.

Dr. Charles had the stock on this gun shortened and narrowed to resemble more of a youth size stock. Worn areas on the gun told us that he used it a lot, and dropped it once or twice.

One of the triggers had been replaced and the other was well worn. This gun was obviously special to Dr. Greenwell. He had it repaired when needed, modified to fit him better, and kept up on preventative maintenance.

As the dark began to settle in we put our fire out and walked back to the truck. Little Joey asked if he could one day have that gun, and I assured him it would be his first one.

On the way home he continued to talk about his Great Grandfather and asking questions about him. Some of these questions I had to make phone calls to get the answers to them.

Dr. Charles has been dead almost 40 years and I never met him.

Most of what I know is because of that gun. It tells its own story and sparks new questions to be answered.

The gun isn't worth much to a prospective buyer, but it's priceless to us.

Hopefully in 30 years Little Joey can sit on a log and introduce his son to his Great, Great-Great Grandfather and hopefully get some squirrels.

Joey Greenwell helps his dad make soap.

CHAPTER 46 **HOW TO MAKE YOUR OWN LAUNDRY DETERGENT**

By Joey Greenwell
The Chesapeake

This past weekend, I made a fresh batch of homemade laundry detergent from a recipe my mom Leslie gave us. I enjoyed the process – I got to make a giant bucket of slime in the kitchen and my kids and wife had a blast. Let's see what we can learn from the process that might save us some cash.

Making the Laundry Detergent

The only ingredients you actually need for homemade laundry detergent are as follows:

1 cup washing soda (I use Arm & Hammer)

1/2 cup borax (I use 20 Mule Team)

1 bar soap (I used dove, but I we used scent free hunters soap it would save $ on scent free detergent)

Approximately 3 gallons water

You'll also need a container of some sort to store this in (I use a five gallon bucket with a lid), something to stir it (I use a large wooden spoon), another pot to boil soapy water in (I use one big enough to hold about ten cups), and something to cut up the soap (I use a cheese grater).

First thing, put about four cups of water into the pan and put it on the stove on high until it's at boiling, then lower the heat until it's simmering.

While it's heating up, take a bar of soap and cut it up into little bits. I found a lot of successes using our box grater, which resulted in a ton of little soap curls.

When the water is boiling, start throwing in the soap. I recommend just doing a bit at a time, then stirring it until it's dissolved.

Stir the soapy water with a spoon until all of the soap is dissolved. Eventually, the water will take on the color of the soap you added, albeit paler. I used Dove soap for this, which was a white soap that looked a lot like a bar of Ivory.

In the end, you'll have some very warm soap soup:

Next, get out your large container and add three gallons of warm tap water to it. I'm using a bright orange five-gallon bucket that I had lying around:

To this bucket add a cup of the washing soda and the soap solution you made and stir. The borax is optional – some people say that it's too harsh, but I've always found that it did a good job getting clothes clean and fresh smelling, so I recommend adding a half cup of borax to the mix.

After stirring, you'll have a bucket full of vaguely soapy water:

Don't worry about the color – it varies depending on what kind of soap you use. I made a batch with Lever 2000 in the past and it had a greenish tint to it, and I've heard reports of all kinds of different colors from other people who have tried this.

At this point, let the soap sit for 24 hours, preferably with a lid on it. I just took our bucket to the laundry room.

When you take off the lid, you'll find any number of things, depending on the type of soap you used and the water you used. It might be firm, like Jello; it might be very watery; it might even be like liquid laundry detergent. Just stir it up a bit and it's ready to be used.

My batch wound up being rather slimy. It had some slimy-feeling water with various sized pieces of white gelatinous stuff floating in it. Here's what it looked like – I'm using a video here because images don't really capture it.

The Cost Breakdown

Here's what I paid for the ingredients…

The box of Borax, which contains enough Borax for at least twelve batches of detergent, cost $2.89. The box of washing soda, which contains enough soda for six batches of detergent, cost $1.89. The soap, which came in packs of three (as pictured above), cost $0.89 per pack – I bought two, to ensure I had enough for six batches. The Iowa sales tax on this stuff was $0.39, giving me a total bill of $6.95 for the ingredients – enough for six batches. I also used perhaps a penny's worth of water and a penny's worth of heat to heat it – a total cost of $6.97.

Each batch of detergent contains 52 cups of the solution – 48 from the three gallons in the bucket, and four more cups of water with the dissolved soap. Since I use one cup per load, this means a single batch makes 52 loads' worth of detergent.

Let's say, hypothetically, that I make six batches of the stuff and use the other half of the box of Borax for something else. That means I've made enough detergent for 312 loads of laundry for a total cost of $6.97. That's roughly two and a quarter cents per load of laundry.

Let's look up Tide with Bleach Alternative, the Consumer Reports recommended detergent. You can buy four bottles of the 150 ounce Tide with Bleach Alternative from Amazon for $62.60. We'll assume free shipping and no taxes here to help Tide's case out. Each of those Tide bottles has enough detergent for 78 loads of laundry, meaning the case will cover 312 loads of laundry. Thus, each load of laundry using Tide with Bleach Alternative costs almost exactly twenty cents ($.20)

I can assure you that we have been using this detergent for a while now and love it! Whatever soap you use is the smell the detergent will take on. So all you hunters out there, use a bar of scent free body soap and you won't have to buy the outrageously price scent free detergent!

The Elizabeth S head boat used to sail from Solomon's Island. The CHESAPEAKE photo

Returning to port from a day on the Bay. THE CHESAPEAKE photo

Colonial Beach, Virginia. Restaurants attract boaters from Maryland. THE CHESAPEAKE photo

CHAPTER 47
HUNTING NEAR HALLOWEEN IN SOUTHERN MARYLAND CAN GET KIND OF SPOOKY

By Rich Johnson
The Chesapeake

I can remember trekking down my old hunting trail at 3 AM on a moonless night with my flashlight off so that I did not spook the deer. As I neared the steel gate on the old fire road, I was startled by something screeching at me off to my right. It sounded like it was coming from a nearby tree off the trail. It may have been an Eastern Screech Owl that was yelling at me, but when you are alone in the pitch dark woods, your imagination can play tricks on you. Well, I stood still for a couple of minutes so to figure out what in the darkness was screeching at me, but I heard no movement or any more screeching. I continued down the old fire road with no more encounters.

To this day, I still don't know what that was screeching at me in the early morning, and makes for a good story. Hunting in Southern Maryland can be pretty spooky considering our past history like the War of 1812 that occurred near here with the British attacking us, pirates attacking the early settlers at Point Patience on the Patuxent River, and the Point Lookout Civil War prison where so many Confederate soldiers died. With so much conflict going on around here, there is bound to be something out there not at rest.

Oh, did I mention that there is Hunting (no early season) at Point Lookout State Park. Sign in is required or call for more information 301-872-5688. Now you can hunt there if you don't mind the ghosts. We all have had the problem of setting up our stand only to have other uninvited folks wondering through the woods spooking your game. Now you may have an uninvited ghost spooking the game and yourself. I have been to Point Lookout for the yearly ghost walk held near Halloween and talked to folks who claim to have seen the ghost orbs of light wandering down a long-abandoned trail, with some taking the shape of a person. Now if you can see the spooks, so can the game making hunting kind of difficult.

Now if the ghosts don't get you, Bigfoot might pay you a visit too. Oh, I forgot to mention that Maryland is rated 5th on the number of sightings of Bigfoot, with the last reported in 2008. So far there have been 26 sightings in Maryland, with most of them occurring in Anne Arundel County. Saint Mary's county seems to be lucky so far with no reported sightings of this critter, for now.

Maryland hunters have had encounters with Bigfoot and not always pleasant. A bow hunter said in 2005 that while Fall hunting deer in the swamp bottoms of West River in Churchton, Maryland (about 40 miles north from Saint Mary's) that he heard some gibberish hollering coming from behind his deer blind about 100 yards away. He said he then smelled the beast and it was like damp, musty road kill with a touch of dirty diapers. This sounds like the sulphur smell many reports when encountering this critter. This hunter quickly left his deer blind with his arrow still ready to shoot, only to have this critter follow him all the way to his car. The hunter estimated the Bigfoot got to within 25 yards of him, and still managed to keep hidden in the thick brush.

Whether you are dealing with Ghosts or this Bigfoot fellow, it can really hamper your hunt. Get that deer, don't get Spooked and be safe.

Chelly Scala and Travis with a prize wild turkey. Photo by Steve Scala

CHAPTER 48
BEFORE TALKING SEX TO A GOBBLER, IT IS A GOOD IDEA TO DO SOME PRE-SCOUTING

By Rich Johnson
The Chesapeake

It is always a good idea to do some Pre-Scouting on whatever Game you plan to hunt, and Spring Gobbler is no different. I did such scouting with my young son last Sunday, and even if you do not see anything, it is a good Father and Son (or Daughter) outing in the woods.

My son will be 5 in June, and like any young boy, he was drawn to every puddle on the trail. It was a good thing I got him some waterproof hunting boots so he did not get water logged. We did some Hen calls asking for a date but did not hear any interested Gobblers.

I suspect it was too early in the season, for the previous night temperatures were still on the chilly side. You see, warmer Springtime temperatures are the norm to get these birds in the Romantic Mood. The trek in the woods was not a total loss for I did see some Turkey droppings which showed their presence. We did jump a deer while we scouted which is good for the youth to see such wildlife.

Now the other good thing with Pre-Scouting is that it checks out your Hunting equipment. You will be surprised how things get after the last time you hunted. My hunting binoculars had a loose strap screw that holds the strap to the binoculars. It is better now that you find that, then your first hunting day.

My Turkey call also had some dry rotted rubber bands that help to hold the call cover on for consistent call control.

Though rubber band replacement is an easy fix, better get this done now than rummaging through your house in the early hours of a hunt and having your wife wonder why you are making so much noise. Remember, women like their sleep, and when Mom is not happy, everyone will suffer. If that was not enough, I could not find my chalk which is used on the call for proper call pitch. Trust me; Pre-Scouting helps out in more ways than you might think.

The other thing Pre-Scouting is good for is determining how the bugs are or will be when you are hunting. Being early, you may not see many bugs, but you can predict. In particular, if there is a lot of standing water, you had better prepare for mosquitoes.

Also to notice is how the tick population is doing. I cannot over preach this "Lyme Disease" is not good and you need to take precautions.

When I took my young son in the woods, I tucked his pants into his boots, and his long sleeve shirt in his pants.

I then sprayed bug spray all over him. Whatever you use, make sure it has Deet in it for this seems to keep them off.

During our trek in the woods, I would monitor our legs to determine if the ticks were starting to climb our legs. In past treks in the woods, I showed my son how ticks climb up on tall grass and wait for an animal to pass by to catch a ride.

He remembered this on this last trek in the woods which is a good thing for he is becoming a woodsman. This early pre-scout, I did not see many ticks but did get one on me. It is always a good idea to take off your shirt and pants (where appropriate) so you can look for the ticks on your clothing.

Better nab these critters now, then having them pounce on you later. I highly recommend getting, if you don't have one yet, a bug net on your head. I have a camouflage hat that has the bug net on the rim and is concealed.

So if I get bugs annoying me, I can pull the bug net down so I can concentrate on Spring Gobbler hunting, vice swatting bugs and letting Mr. Tom know where I am.

Being comfortable during hunting is crucial no matter what Game you are after. If the bugs are annoying you, this will make for a miserable hunt and also diminish your chances of getting a Gobbler for your swatting will give you position away.

So do some pre-scouting for your Spring Gobbler season with your Son or Daughter. It will help you bond with your child, plus teach them valuable woodsman skills. Of course, your equipment will be verified ready for the hunt and how bad the bugs will be. Good Luck in you Spring Gobbler hunt.

CHAPTER 49
BOATING HAS NEVER BEEN CHEAPER

By Ken Rossignol
The Chesapeake

Boating has never been less expensive to get into in decades as it is now and a cruise through the internet will show literally thousands of boats to choose from, with lots of beautiful boats available for a fraction of their value.

For boaters in the Southern Maryland region a visit to local marinas will find 'for sale' signs galore and whether shopping on the internet or in boatyards, the term 'buyer beware' is the chief phrase to remember in addition to the old cliché about a boat being a hole in the water surrounded by wood into which one throws money.

While that money is not likely to be seen again, having a boat allows a tremendous amount of freedom and fun and the Southern Maryland area is wide open for boaters.

Those who have spent warm weather months on the middle or upper Chesapeake will be astounded to see so few boats out on the local rivers and Bay.

It's hard to imagine that there are likely 100 million people who live within a four-hour drive of the middle of the Potomac River. One can travel for an hour on the Potomac and if it's late afternoon on a Sunday, nary a vessel will pass.

Aside from shopping for great deals on used boats and even new ones, as many boat dealers have gone out of business and the banks who own their former inventory are anxious to find buyers to bail them out of their reacquired merchandise, good deals can be found on bulletin boards at grocery stores, tackle shops or in the workplace.

Families who have lost part of the family income are often looking to divest themselves of a boat for which they have no ability to keep up the payments and the down payments they have made may have reduced the

equity and lowered the payoff. Some lenders will allow a new buyer to assume the loan after passing credit checks.

Other boats have been paid off and are being sold to rid an estate of an unwanted expense as many boats have to be kept in marinas and even when stored on land, monthly storage fees add up. All of these factors tend to motivate sellers and the deals around the marketplace now are astounding.

Therefore, while many homeowners in the country are 'underwater' on their mortgages, the same applies to boat owners with hefty payments.

If you see a boat you like, make a ridiculous offer and you will likely end up as the owner.

Some larger sailboats and cabin cruisers lend themselves to be 'liveaboards', but be sure the marina which is housing the boat you are interested will allow 'liveaboards'. Check this out before buying that great boat you intend on making your home.

But with the dismal economy rocking marinas as well, expect more flexibility from the marina owners. Even though a boat may seem solid, the best assurance for a new buyer is to haul it out of the water and take a look at the bottom. For novice boaters, the employment of a marine surveyor could make an investment in a pricey cruiser, trawler or sailboat well worth the fee.

In many cases, insurance companies will require an inspection from a surveyor and if you buy the boat, it might be a good time to go ahead and paint the bottom and replace the zincs while it's out of the water.

Living aboard a boat can be a really fun life when compared to the cost of condos in the Washington area and marinas near and in the District have many live-aboard opportunities while those in the Southern Maryland area tend to discourage them.

Marinas with septic systems on public sewer usually are more receptive and once again the rule book may be tossed aside in this current market as marinas are eager for any income.

Even those marinas which do not allow full-time residency still make your boat your weekend and vacation retreat which many boaters remember fondly as some of the best times of their lives.

Unscrupulous marina owners and managers can be tough to deal with after you have already signed up for a slip rental and it's a good idea to walk around the docks and chat with folks in a marina before you make up your mind to rent a slip. Most boat owners will be diplomatic about the marina but will still give clues as to what to expect.

Many marinas do not allow boat owners to bring in outside vendors to work on their boats and these marinas are usually forthright about their policy. In most cases, those mechanics can be pretty good ones and the policy might be doing you a favor.

But there are still boatyards around which will allow you to do any of the work yourself.

Again, 'buyer beware' and before having a boatyard do work for you, check out their customer satisfaction level.

The more expensive boatyards and marinas usually have their rules prominently available and have been around the barn a few times, thus tend to have worked out how to run the yard in order to make a profit and yet at the same time make their customers happy.

What size boat you buy and what kind to buy depends on your abilities and your wallet.

Some folks can handle an old wooden skiff, but they tend to be heavy and require a lot of bailing to keep them from sinking. That means being around after a heavy rain or if you don't bail them, you may soon own a submarine.

Trailing a boat works fine for many folks, and in St. Mary's County there are nearly two dozen boat ramps for the estimated 10,000 registered small boats on trailers.

The Point Lookout boat launching ramp at the State Park and the Solomon's boat launching ramp are two of the biggest in the area. The ramp at the Hallowing Point across from Benedict is a great ramp and the

Abell's Wharf, Chaptico Wharf, Bushwood Wharf and Piney Point ramps are all popular with local residents and visitors who manage to learn where they are located.

The options for those who live on the water are more plentiful including piers with boat lifts and slips or even private ramps.

Canoes can be launched at the Macintosh Run in Leonardtown and at the Great Mills launching ramp on the upper St. Mary's River at Great Mills. Both of these locations are on Rt. 5. At Leonardtown, there is now a vendor who will rent canoes and kayaks.

These two launching areas allow for parking and canoes can be paddled for a remarkable trip down scenic vistas.

Most weekends will see Amish and Mennonite youths and families pulling canoes on wagons behind their buggies, loaded down with coolers and fishing gear for overnight camping.

Even on windy days when the open rivers are too rough for small boats, these launching areas can propel the paddlers into miles of calmer waters for exercise and touring that one would never see from larger boats that cannot navigate the shallower waters of the St. Mary's River headwaters or Macintosh Run on its trip down to Breton Bay.

Water skiing and tubing abound on the larger bays like St. Clements and Breton Bay as well as the open stretches of the Patuxent, the Potomac, St. Mary's and Wicomico.

Speed limits in creeks prohibit water skiing even when common sense doesn't slow speed boats down.

On the Potomac, a private island, known as Sharks Tooth Island sells memberships by the year. A sign is prominently displayed on the island with a phone number to call for paying the membership fee. There are reports of the island being an excellent place to push the boat close to shore and anchor for swimming and picnicking.

Many of those who become members of one of the world's most exclusive clubs, and perhaps most remote, pitch canopies for shade and watch as their children play on the beach.

Others water-ski from the island and memberships are mandatory as the owner enforces the no-trespassing for non-members, although it has been reported that one-day passes can be had in exchange for a bottle of whiskey.

Sailing is an art and requires skill, training, and patience. Those who enjoy sailing are the original budget boaters as the wind blows free but finicky as to when it appears.

Still, those who enjoy sailing have their favorite vessels and there have been many folks in Southern Maryland who have circumnavigated the world after leaving their own dock, as long-time resident and sailor Jack Witten did about 25 years ago.

Catamaran owners Larry and Clare Whitbeck dream about such a trip and are gradually gaining the skills need to carry them to distant islands.

The sailing associations in the area which sponsor weekly races and regattas offer an entirely different dimension to boating from those who fish, paddle and water ski.

Boaters who fail to exercise due caution when buying a boat, falling in love with the concept and failing to consider the consequences, can still reap enough pleasure from some of the biggest mistakes to make it all worthwhile.

One soul who spotted a great deal on a wooden 1957 Owens cabin cruiser with twin slant six Dodge engines for a mere $2,000, which ran like a charm, and he forgot about the 'old check the bottom deal'. That boat owner had got lots of fun for two seasons before rough weather revealed the flaws in the keel and the old girl was soon put up on land for a bonfire and its engines salvaged. To this day, the handsome Owens wheel is in the pilothouse of that boat owner's fiberglass cabin cruiser.

The region is host to the venerable Corinthian Yacht Club, formed in 1903, with a 20 acre facility rooted in a fine location near Wynne on Jutland Creek after moving from Washington, D.C. more than 50 years ago. Corinthian offers its members a fine layout of covered and uncovered slips in a protected cove with easy access out to the best fishing grounds. With a clubhouse, swimming pool and rental cabins, along with monthly activities, the club's mostly power boat owners organize various cruises during the course of the season.

Trips up and down the Bay and the rivers are as varied as anyone's interests and this column will explore adventures on the water, dining at Southern Maryland's great waterfront seafood joints and all aspects of boating life.

The *Poppa Francis* on display at the Leonardtown Waterfront Festival. The buyboat is fully operational and is open for viewing at such events. THE CHESAPEAKE photo

CHAPTER 50
NEW LIFE FOR AN OLD ROD

By Cap'n Larry Jarboe
The Chesapeake

Likely, you have a favorite rod that you've had for a lifetime or maybe a rod that your Dad owned and you still use. Years of salt spray, sun baking, and general wear probably show the age of your favorite fishing tool. An eye or two might be missing, but this is still the go to rod for most of your fishing expeditions.

Jim Wood in his Breezy Point Custom Rod shop in Ridge is ready to fix up your favorite old rod. THE CHESAPEAKE photo

Imagine, the same rod with a fresh handle, new guides, anodized reel seat, shiny wraps and high gloss finish. This work of art is ready for another generation of fishing tales that can be created by your very own magic wand rigged with a matching reel.

Bluntly speaking, most of us do not have the time, patience, equipment, or finesse to expertly refurbish a classic fishing stick or custom build a new rod. Fortunately, there are artisans among us willing to take on this labor of love without charging an arm and a leg.

With the cold weather locked in, it is time to plan for next year's fishing adventures. This is a good time to get that favorite rod refurbished or plan to have a custom rod built for your unique requirements.

I spent a very informative afternoon in Jim Wood's toasty warm custom rod workshop at Breezy Point in Ridge. Do you know how the spine is positioned in a rod? How do you determine how many eyes are needed on a rod? How many coats of epoxy are required to smooth out the fresh wraps on a rod?

Jim will share all that knowledge with you as well as making sure your favorite worn out fishing stick gets a new life, brighter and more efficient than ever before.

In Southern Maryland, we are fortunate to have many craftsmen who fill specialized niches in our community. At the CHESAPEAKE, we are always looking for those exceptional people and businesses who rise above the Wal-Mart philosophy to produce heirloom goods and quality services.

Outfitting a rod crafted and signed by Jim Wood while sitting beside a warm wood stove in January or February will make the winter pass a little faster and the fishing to come even more fun.

St. Mary's County, Md., County Commissioner President Randy Guy with Cap'n Larry Jarboe and a boat load of fish.

Chapter 50 John Wilkes Booth's Pocketknife

By Stephen G. Uhler
The Chesapeake

I recently did a land-clearing job in Charles County's Zekiah Valley. We had to take out several big white oaks, and they presented me with a problem. What to do with the felled trees?

Not worth hauling to a sawmill, stump dumps would charge a fortune for the privilege of dumping them. I couldn't burn them where they were.

They would make some fine firewood, but I already have enough firewood piled in my yard to last the next three generations.

Finally, I realized that I would just have to saw them into firewood and haul them to my yard and add to the glut of firewood already there.

I decided I would go get the wood on the first available Saturday, but first I would need to find a partner in the enterprise. I am reluctant to work in the woods alone, I have been injured too many times. I figured if I sawed my leg off and bled to death it would be nice to have someone to call the coroner.

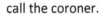

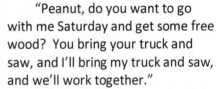

"Peanut, do you want to go with me Saturday and get some free wood? You bring your truck and saw, and I'll bring my truck and saw, and we'll work together."

"Yes suh, 'deed I do need some wood."

We were making a nice day of it. The saws were in tune, the air was pleasantly brisk. We were going to have two big loads of wood before the sun went down.

Then, "sking!" My saw hit a piece of metal in the log. That's some bad luck hitting a piece of metal with a chain saw. It just about ruins your chain.

Oh sure, I can file away at a bent tooth and make it saw pretty well, but you can never get it to cut perfectly after hitting a metal object like that.

The cut that I was making in the log would have been six or seven feet from the ground while the tree was still standing. It couldn't be a fence staple, nobody would have had a fence that tall.

I decided to chip away with my axe to find out just what I had struck.

I chipped away carefully until I had exposed enough of the object to discover that it was a penknife. A penknife with a fancy silver handle. The two steel blades had rusted away to dust, but the slightly tarnished case was still in just about perfect condition.

From the diameter of the log, I knew that the knife had been left there a long time ago.

As I exposed a little more of the beautifully engraved silver handle, I saw what looked to be initials.

With a little spit and rubbing the initials were brought to view.

J.W.B.

Holy mackerel, I have found John Wilkes Booth's pocketknife, the same knife he used to cut away the bunting that fouled his broken leg, the same knife he brandished while exiting Ford's Theatre.

Wow! This relic is worth a fortune. I didn't let 'Peanut' notice what I had found. It was bad enough having to share all this firewood with him, I didn't' want him to claim a share of my valuable trophy.

I decided to confirm the date of my find by counting the annual rings surrounding the knife.

Yep. 137 rings. The knife was left in the fork of a young white oak in the year 1865. In fact, the knife's position in the first quarter of the 137th ring would date it to April 1865.

Now, for the sake of argument, you could say the knife belonged to J. W. Bowling or perhaps Joe Willie Bassford, who resided in these environs circa 1865.

But, let me rebut, both of those men were subsistence tobacco farmers. They surely carried pocketknives, but the knife of a poor farmer would have a handle of bone or horn and not finely engraved sterling silver.

The knife I had found belonged to a gentleman of wealth and fame.

I stopped chipping at the knife, thinking that if I presented it to the experts still buried within the log, with the stump still in the ground, that the experts would immediately authenticate it as John Wilkes Booth's knife.

It was known that Booth left Dr. Mudd's house five or six miles from here and that this trail I was on would be a direct line to his rendezvous with his co-conspirator at Faulkner.

This tree was just at the distance a wounded, fast fleeing rider would stop to rest his bones and give his horse a blow.

He probably would have needed to tighten the saddle on his sweaty horse, and used the knife to cut away knotted rawhide in his cinch strap.

The logical thing for a man to do while cutting away sweaty girth ties and re-lacing them would be to free his hands by laying his knife on the nearest shelf (or, in this case, tree crotch).

Even if the professors at the Smithsonian did not validate my find, I would always know that I owned the knife that was carried by the man who killed Lincoln.

I didn't want to draw the attention of that greedy 'Peanut' to my million-dollar find and casually threw my precious block in our pile of firewood. I could pick it out later at home.

But when I unloaded my blocks the one with the knife was nowhere to be found.

I burnt rubber to 'Peanut's' house.

"Where's my block?"

"Come on man, you ain't gonna fight about dividing up the wood. You got a bigger load than I did."

"I don't care how much wood you got or didn't get. There was one particular ford grained block that I wanted for...uh...uh 'Furniture wood'."

"Man, you couldn't use that piece for any furniture; it had a piece of 'arn' in it. I seen it and didn't want it to get to my saw so I split it out, took it straight in the house and throwed it in the fire."

"Dammit Peanut, that wasn't just a piece of iron, that was John Wilkes Booth's Knife."

"Man, you losing your mind. Bootsie Wilkinson wasn't even with us. There was just me and you."

"I didn't say, Bootsie Wilkinson, you dyslexic, little bastard, I said John Wilkes Booth."

"He wasn't with us neither."

'Peanut' led me to his stove it was still hot. I began raking the coals out on his floor. I was so mad at that point I didn't care if his shack burned to the ground.

There it is, at the bottom of the stove. Not the beautifully engraved knife that I had left in the log but a nondescript puddle of sterling silver, a Rorschach blob of melted silver worth about $2.00 down at the junkyard.

Why did I have to team up with that miserable bastard? Why didn't I just grab my million-dollar find and leave him in the woods? Why? Why? My last chance at fame and fortune gone up in smoke.

I carried that little chunk of silver around in my pocket, refusing to part with; no one else will ever know its value.

But, I knew that little blob of metal was once held in the hand that held the gun that assassinated a president.

Then one night in a bar I was fishing in my pocket for some coins and absentmindedly laid the blob of silver on the bar.

"What you carrying that around for?" some wise ass asked.

"That, sir, was once the knife of John Wilkes Booth."

"Oh yeah, sure, do you see this ring on my finger? It was once worn in the belly-button of Princess Diana. She gave it to me while we were carrying on our torrid affair."

The bar broke out with jeers and laughter. I stumbled out into the night determined never to be so humiliated again.

Maybe I should put it in a safe, or maybe just give it to my grandsons for a curio.

But no, it would only resurface years from now to embarrass them!

I drove down to Clarkes Landing and hurled that piece of s--- as far into the Patuxent as my arm could throw it. What is the sense of keeping a priceless relic if you can't prove it is a priceless relic?

Margaret and Paul Raley, James Wilson, Dorothy and Jr. Photo courtesy of Cue Ball Raley. Location: St. Inigoes, Md.

CHAPTER 51 **BAG YOUR TROPHY ROCK FOR A BUCK**

Cap'n Larry Jarboe
The Chesapeake

The best way to guarantee to catch a trophy rockfish is to fish with a pro. The price for a six passenger charter boat is usually around six hundred bucks. How can a single buck ensure that you have one or more big fish to brag about with pictures and a freezer full of filets as proof?

If you squirrel away a buck a day for fishing adventures, you will accumulate 365 dollars a year to apply toward fishing with your favorite charter captain. Find five other fishing fanatics willing to do the same and you will have enough funding for three trips, tips included.

Personally, I am not too proud to admit that I am a lousy trolling fisherman. My specialty is catching fish with bait and, in many cases, the liberal application of chum. I can hold my own live baiting, jigging, and chucking lures, but trolling is my weakness. Plus, I like the peace and quiet of a boat at anchor or adrift with the engine shut down.

If you're going to catch those big striped bass that prowl the Chesapeake, you will most likely be trolling a lot of big lures, teasers, parachute rigs, and planer combos. Just decking out the proper gear and quality trolling rigs can cost well over a thousand dollars. Add a couple hundred bucks in fuel for a day's trolling with the big outboard and that charter boat looks like a pretty good deal. Throw in the working captain's daily experience and it's better to fish close to home with your boat but pay the pro's price for a day on the Bay.

My first big rockfish was caught on a cold early December day when the wind was screaming at 25 knots from the WNW. Capt. Greg Madjeski who fishes the Temple M out of Ridge suggested that we try the lee side of the Potomac River prior to battling across the Bay. The fall run stripers should be on the Virginia side of the channel not far from the dock.

Sure enough in less than a half hour, the first rod doubled over. On the way out, we had drawn cards for pole position. Since I drew the Ace of Spades, I was assured to get the first shot at one of those big fish.

While cranking in the first fish, it dropped off the line. If looks could kill, I'd be dead, but Capt. Greg got back on the fish and our whole party of six each got a big fish. Even I got a second chance which this time came into the boat. We were maxed out for our limit of striped bass over 28 inches before 9 A.M.

Capt. Greg proceeded to set his course to cross the Bay in search of six smaller rock and, maybe, some sea trout. I suggested that we had witnessed a phenomenal day of fine fishing. Instead of beating ourselves and the boat in rough open water, why not enjoy our success with an early trip back to the dock for a cold beer?

Everyone in our party agreed and I think Capt. Greg forgave me for missing that first fish.

What a wonderful charter fishing trip we had. I am saving my bucks for the next one.

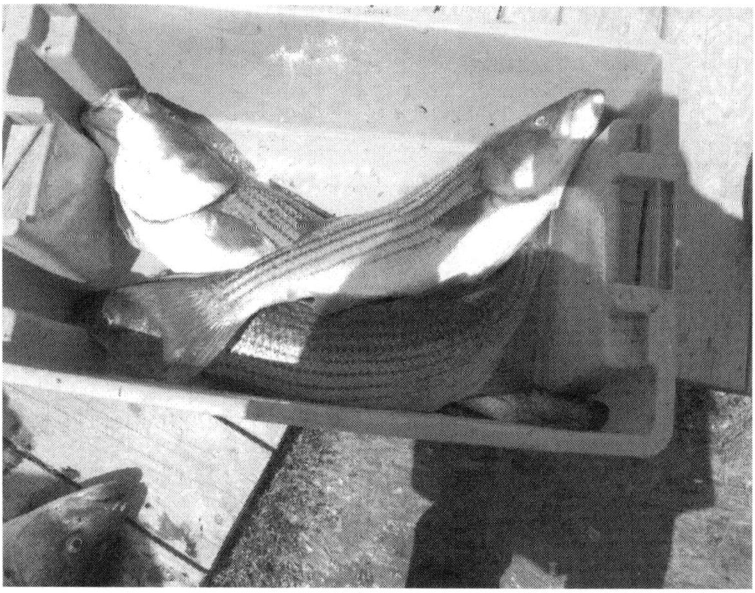

Why you should go fishing from Buzz's Marina in Ridge, Md. The proof is in the cooler. THE CHESAPEAKE

ABOUT THE CHESAPEAKE

Join us as we visit the best of The Chesapeake for action, fun and adventure in The Chesapeake region. Murder, Mayhem and Mystery along with blues, rockfish, and Serendipity Serenades to convince fish to jump onto the hook.

From Jack Rue, Fred McCoy and Pepper Langley come great stories about the Twentieth Century in Southern Maryland, from the Potomac to the Patuxent. Learn about the early days of the Patuxent River Naval Air Station and the boomtown of Lexington Park, called the Walled City. From Lou Clements to Steven Gore Uhler, our collection of short stories is sure to keep you entertained. Cap'n Larry Jarboe's expertise in fish stories knows no equal!

ThePrivateerClause.com

Ken@ThePrivateerClause.com

ENTER TODAY with EMAIL address for a chance to win a FREE PAPERWHITE KINDLE or choice of a $119 gift card at Amazon or other great prize!

Visit ThePrivateerClause.com and submit name and email address and win a free Kindle book along with a chance to win a great new Paperwhite or a gift card at the end of our special promotion.

Unlike tablets, Kindle Paperwhite is designed to deliver a superior reading experience.

BE SURE TO SIGN UP FOR OUR EMAIL LIST

Moreover, GET ANOTHER BOOK FREE

www.ThePrivateerClause.com

Available in paperback and Audible at Amazon and retailers worldwide

The Marsha & Danny Jones Thrillers

1 The Privateer Clause

#2 Return of the Sea Empress
#3 Follow Titanic
#4 Follow Triangle – Vanish!
#5 Cruise Killer
#6 BEHEADED – Terror By Land, Sea & Air

Additional books by Ken Rossignol

Chesapeake 1850
Chesapeake 1880
Chesapeake 1910 (coming soon)

Battle of Solomon's Island

Titanic Series

Titanic 1912
Titanic & Lusitania- Survivor Stories (with Bruce M. Caplan)
Titanic Poetry, Music & Stories

The Chesapeake Series

The Chesapeake: Tales & Scales (with Larry Jarboe)
The Chesapeake: Legends, Yarns & Barnacles (with Larry Jarboe)

Non-fiction

KLAN: Killing America
Panama 1914
The Story of The Rag
Leopold & Loeb Killed Bobby Franks (with Bruce M. Caplan)

CHESAPEAKE CRIME CONFIDENTIAL

Coke Air: Chesapeake Crime Confidential

PIRACY and PIRATES – Non-fiction

Pirate Trials: Dastardly Deeds & Last Words

Pirate Trials: Hung by the Neck Until Dead

Travel

Fire Cruise

Cruising the Waterfront Restaurants of the Potomac

The Traveling Cheapskate series:

The Ninety-Nine Cent Tour of Bar Harbor Maine

Boating Chesapeake Bay

36168282R00142

Made in the USA
Middletown, DE
25 October 2016